Copyright © 2021

ISBN 978-1-8384583-1-7

Printed by Amazon P.O.D

First printing, 2021.

#firstofthemonthcheckforalump

For my wonderful husband Rob.

I had no idea one person could take on so much at once and be so truly amazing. It was easy to remain positive when he was looking after us all so well. He is a superhero, my iron man and soul mate. There are no words to describe how grateful I am for the unconditional love and support he has given me. I've had his full backing to write this book and he will once again care for everyone if he sees I'm busy with it. I couldn't function without you Rob. Love you RVL1

Jonny, Mya, Ben and Damo…this is also for you. Don't ever forget, whatever you want in life is there for the taking. Only you can make that happen and I believe in each and every one of you. Reach for the stars my amazing children and thank you for all you bring to my life. xx

Table of Contents

Boobs Are For life, Not Just For Insta!

Sarah Vaughan

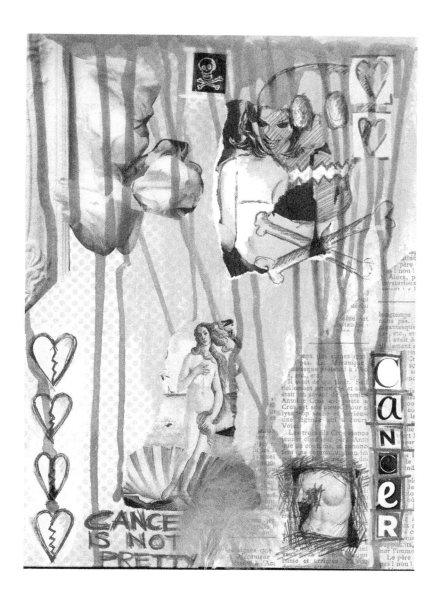

Foreword

What is breast cancer? I can tell you what it isn't. It isn't pink, and it isn't fluffy. It's not feather boas and 'Race for Life' pictures on social media with pink neon face paint. It's brutal, and it's painful. It's veins collapsing, puke, violation, bald bits and endless trips to hospital. It's not dignified, it's debilitating and can be life changing. BUT and I say this with a huge BUT, like my butt after steroids. I was determined not to dwell on the nasty negatives or feel sorry for myself. I felt positive about my battle/journey, whatever you want to call it, and I found using social media and humour (sometimes dark humour, sorry mum) helped me to get through it. So, whilst I don't think cancer is pink, glittery or glamorous, I get people want to support the cause by 'feather boa' fundraising I'm very, very thankful for that. Please don't stop. This pink 'fluffiness', has raised a lot of money which is fundamental in enabling research and finding breakthrough's in treatment. It allows trials and drugs that have probably saved my life and the life of someone you know or are close to.

I have written this book for myself, because if nothing else it will have been cathartic. If it helps anyone with cancer, or anyone supporting a loved one with cancer, then brilliant, job done. If it encourages you to become confident in checking your breasts on a regular basis then I will be ecstatic.

I suppose what I want you to read is an honest, but uplifting idiots' guide, to dealing with breast cancer or supporting friends and family diagnosed with breast cancer.

My key priority is, and has always been, to use my situation to raise awareness and prompt people to get into the habit of checking. I thought I was good at it; turns out I wasn't - was I? Cancer touches us all either directly, or indirectly now unfortunately, and breast cancer at present, affects 1 in 8 women in the UK. Chances are you have had it yourself or watched a loved one go through it and so I hope it may help you. I hope it makes you realise there can be positivity from a diagnosis for so many of us now. With early detection, advances in medicine, treatment and understanding of the disease improving all the time, cancer is very much part of life rather than equating to death.

SHE STOOD
IN THE STORM,
& WHEN THE
WIND DID NOT
BLOW HER WAY,
SHE ADJUSTED
HER SAILS.

ELIZABETH EDWARDS

A Bump in the Road

I was an ordinary girl living an ordinary life. Then cancer turned this 'ordinary life' upside down.

Born in 1974 to a loving hard-working family, I'd lived a charmed life growing up in sunny St Helens, which for those of you whose never had the privilege to visit is a fairly large working-class town, nestled between Liverpool and Manchester. Salubrious it is not, but there is a warmth and passion that is glossed over by its critics, who prefer to focus only on the varied selection of charity and pound shops that make up the now neglected town centre. I liked it enough to return at aged 35, after living away for seventeen years.

I lived a nomadic life when I left to go to university in 1992. Living in Lincoln, Carlisle, London, Brighton and Shoreham. Collecting fab memories, friends and even a husband and child by the time I returned to St Helens in 2009.

My daughter went from having a cheeky little southern accent, living close to the sea and wanting to count ALL the pebbles on Shoreham beach, to our new life, living with my parents, whilst we renovated our house and she loved it. She got lots of attention (and chocolate) and a newly decorated 'big girls' bedroom. She was precious. Because of endometriosis, I'd struggled to conceive and required various Laparoscopies to diagnose, and laser away, the scar tissue that caused two years of infertility. Thankfully, she came along after a difficult labour, which ended with her being stuck or stubborn, I still haven't worked out which. So, she arrived out of the sunroof (emergency c-section) along with the departure of 2.5 litres of my blood. Still, we'd created a life, and the NHS had saved mine, so all was well.

I'd worked as an art teacher since 1996, and so I was delighted on my return 'home' to slot into a job teaching in a small unit for students with complex and medical needs. Over the next few years, I was not delighted to experience four miscarriages and the trauma they bring. I've never been totally open about them, preferring to just put them in the past and move forward. This is partly because of self-preservation and partly because I felt shame in thinking I failed to do the one thing I was put on this earth for. I now feel strongly that the unwritten code to wait until the 12th week to be open about pregnancy causes a woman to feel shame should the pregnancy not progress. Effectively you go through the hardest trimester in secret and then should the pregnancy end you are almost obliged to hide the pain too.

To go through this time and time again without a reason felt cruel, demoralising and so emotionally painful. Why is it women's health issues are often hidden or taboo? Looking back, they were tricky times, and I didn't much like the cloud I carried around with me during this period of my life. I became an expert at the painted smile and turning off my feelings like a tap. It wasn't an Oscar worthy performance but there was a definite 'keep calm and carry on' attitude, without addressing some hurt this had caused.

After a lot of soul searching, we decided that adoption was the path someone destined us to walk, and although a difficult and intrusive process, it was one of the best decisions of my life.

It took a while to be assessed and approved (as it should) but finally, as a family, we could share the love we had with a child who would become our own and a brother to Mya. The fairy-tale life would be complete, and that cold rainy March brought me my whirlwind. I never looked back.

To be fair, once he was walking, he was pretty good at running off, so I never got the chance to look back. Those early days and months were hard, and it took me a while to 'love' my little boy. Don't judge me, the love isn't instant and doesn't happen overnight; no matter how much you convince yourself it will. His story was not tragic but wasn't simple either. Now I forget I didn't give birth to him; he is just part of me and our family.

Unfortunately, the change to our family was the catalyst to the breakdown of my relationship with my then husband and we separated. This resulted in divorce and a stint as a single mum. An interesting, if not a lonely and challenging time. I would often cry on my way into work after mornings from hell, trying to get my shit together. I hadn't realised how capable I could be and although it brought challenges; I was actually, without realising it, in training for what was to come.

Health wise, I was always the first to pick up germs and often had colds or coughs. Other than those miscarriages and being prone to benign breast lumps, I was fit and healthy and thankful for it. I had dabbled with running over the years and was thrilled I had the stamina and determination to train for a marathon (the same year of my diagnosis) and ran 26.2 miles around Barcelona with my running club teammates. Somehow, I even ran four half marathons that year, one of which was two days before my breast clinic appointment (so after I had found the lump). I was more 'Forrest Lump' than Forrest Gump, but the fittest I had been in my life.

2017 was the happiest year. I was in love with a wonderful man, Rob, who had swept me off my feet when I was least expecting it. I think we were the last to know, as having worked together, and annoyed each other for a few years, we had bonded over the difficulties of being a single parent and I suddenly saw in him this caring and supportive friend and it went from there. Next thing we were engaged, moving in together with our families and very smitten. He believed in me and thought I was amazing (and still does!). This love and support made me feel like a better person. I was living the best life and very excited about the future. He had just sold his house and moved his kids into mine and we were about to move into another house we were buying with our new blended family of six.

Apart from work being stressful, I felt very happy, loved and content. I wasn't someone who ever smoked (I won't include smoking a whole pack in a nightclub when I was 18). I've certainly been careful what I ate since my diet of two Twix bars a day when I was at school (don't tell my mum and dad) and was an avid juicer for a while, supplementing an already balanced diet. Although, if I'm honest, not that balanced- Gin and gym, but hey ho, we all have our vices.

Ultimately, I guess what I'm trying to say is, I didn't feel like I had done anything to warrant this stupid disease but to put it into perspective, who wakes up in the morning and deserves to be diagnosed with cancer? If I had smoked, does that mean I deserved to get lung cancer? Or if I had a poor diet, was my penance for colon cancer? Maybe I was just really, really naughty in a former life, who knows?

I'd learnt years earlier that life isn't fair, and you just have to face what they throw at you, whether or not you like it. I was determined to do this, knowing there would be bumps in the road. Unfortunately, now my bump in the road turned out to be a craggy mountain. I was going to dig deep and trek high. And that I did!

Tuesdays Child is full of Face

November the 9th 2017. Whilst lying in bed, I found a really hard mass in my right boob. It felt like being engorged when you breastfeed and it surprised me, but I wasn't worried. I'd had four previous visits to the breast clinic thanks to my 'breast mice' (nickname for a Fibroadenoma) one of which, I'd had removed, and all the others disappeared, as they tend to. I knew the drill: Go to the GP and get referred, examination, ultrasound, mammogram, land biopsy. Get told it's a harmless Fibroadenoma/cyst. Go home relieved. Or so I thought...

Alas, the wonders of the NHS. I got straight on the Patient access app on my phone and got myself an appointment for the following afternoon. I didn't bat an eyelid when she examined me, and within minutes I was back in the car and would await the referral to the breast unit. My appointment was for the afternoon of Tuesday, the 21st of November. I was told to leave up to three hours to allow for various tests. But familiarity breeds 'content' and I was still blasé: "It won't take 3 hours; it's probably an infected milk duct or a cyst and let's face it, I know everything, and it won't happen to me." We didn't even make plans for the school run, as I was convinced we would be done and dusted by then.

My colleagues knew where I was going and knew I was not concerned. That's because I wasn't, I'd totally played it down.

It's grim in the waiting room of the Burney Breast unit (named after Fanny Burney 'Ouch'! How unfortunate) and busy, very busy. As usual, until I saw a friend in there, I was the youngest by at least 20 years. It's one of those situations where no one wants to make eye contact but you can tell people want to know why you are there, more for reassurance than anything else, as we all asked ourselves, "Has everyone here got cancer?"

The clock told me I'd been waiting too long, and I was getting nervous, as people who came in after me have been called through several times now and it reminded me that I hate the place. I felt vulnerable and wanted to feel in control. Ironically, this is the most in control I would feel for many months, but obviously I didn't realise this yet.

Eventually my name was read out and I went through to be examined. This was the first sign that something sinister was occurring and I felt like I was looking down on my life rather than living it. Whilst examining me, the nurse found a considerable size lump in my right breast and a pea sized lump in my armpit that I hadn't even noticed. Alarm bells started ringing. I sensed her concern, and it hurt, like really hurt, as she prodded deeply into my sweaty pit and breast tissue. I'm not a soap dodger but the cold sweat from panic was layering my body.

Rob tried to reassure me as she popped out of the room for something, but I'd been here before remember, and this had never happened. Obviously, you're reading this knowing full well what the outcome was, but I was really worried at this point. The next few hours brought a variety of familiar tests which felt intrusive and I was resentful: this was not part of my plan.

The ultrasound isn't uncomfortable and with the help of a bit of local anaesthetic; the biopsies are ok. I have had two types previously: a FNA Fine needle aspiration and a CNB core needle biopsy. The latter isn't a walk in the park, but the local anaesthetic is powerful enough and I know not to listen for the stapler sound when they take the samples of tissue. (Yes, it's toe curling). I was definitely feeling like a lab monkey and in between all these tests I was shepherded back and forth into the waiting 'Room of Doom' to dread the call of my name. There was a mock-up blossom tree with positive messages of hope and recovery hanging from the poster paper branches and without this sounding like a GCSE English essay, my stomach lurched, and I looked away.

Each time they called me, the tension clamping my chest (how apt) grew tighter and tighter and I felt terrified as my intuition was telling me it wasn't good news. This definitely felt different to other experiences I'd had, and it was the absence of confidence towards this being a cyst or Fibroadenoma that filled me with fear. Yet, no one ever used the word cancer or alluded to it. At some point I had encouraged Rob to get the kids from school and ferry them home, or to their various clubs, but it meant he left me alone. Partly, I was still optimistic that I did not need him there and all would be well. At the same time, I was also pre-empting that the news would not be good and wanted to be in control of how I dealt with that, rather than trying to hide it from my Mum and Dad, who would probably be the ones stepping up to sort out the kids.

By the time they called me for the mammogram, I was alone and becoming quite distressed. This time the mammogram was traumatic and honestly, I've never felt pain like it. Squeezing my right boob (with the addition of an avocado size cancer inside) into plates on that bloody machine was torture. The pain radiated through my body and I can remember my toes curling and the tears forming, as I was struggling to catch my breath. The unsympathetic radiographer asked me if I usually have panic attacks (?!

I wanted to scream at her. It was bloody excruciating and the type of pain that makes you feel sick. I know what you are now thinking, I am never having a mammogram it sounds awful! Don't read this and let it put you off. I've had mammograms before and since this experience, and whilst it's uncomfortable, it really isn't that bad. Take a couple of Paracetamol if you have a low pain threshold, but it takes literally seconds and rarely feels like your boobs are being squashed into a hot George Foreman grill. (Other grilling machines are available).

We are lucky to have access to this kind of testing and shouldn't refuse it due to it being uncomfortable. I had a good cry to my friends sitting in the waiting room, as luckily, they were still there (and for them the news was good, thankfully). Having a cry was a good release, even if I got a lot of sympathetic looks from around the 'Room of Doom'.

When they called me in to see the consultant after all my tests, he asked me where my partner had gone, and would I rather wait until he returned before they spoke to me. Even at this point the optimist in me wasn't worried that it was anything serious, as I insisted, I was ok. In that split second, I am thinking of the potential of having my crazy three-year-old in the meeting too. So no, I opted to continue alone.

The consultant (who shall remain nameless, but I am so glad he has retired, as his bedside manner had a lot to be desired), the nurse who examined me, and a Macmillan nurse (yes it felt like an interview), told me they were concerned: I had a significant mass in my right breast and a lump in my lymph nodes. They did not describe it as cancer and kept telling me they would wait for results. I felt we went all around the houses a lot and whilst he was evasive at best, cryptic at worst, I remained clueless

But then the penny was starting to drop, I'm not stupid. Why did we have a Macmillan nurse in there? I'd never had that before. Macmillan means cancer, doesn't it? OH SHIT!

The rest of the meeting was a confusing blur, and I couldn't wait to get out of there as it was clear I would not get a definitive answer, even when I asked, "Ok, so if you won't acknowledge its cancer, then what is it and how will it be treated?"

Louisa, the Macmillan nurse, was lovely. She was supportive, without being overly sympathetic. She took me for a meeting-just the two of us. I was then asked my family and home situation, what my job is, previous health issues and other gentle probing that I can't recall.

Cancer was only skirted around, but there was something in my gut that was ringing alarm bells. I think I asked that if it is cancerous when I will have it removed. I was told that I would probably start Chemotherapy first to shrink it if it is a tumour. I recognised this response and line of treatment has been considered. Protocol must have been not to tell me it's highly likely I had cancer, but Louisa knew. She was also aware what she said to me will play over and over in my mind over the next few weeks, so she carefully chose her words. She knew my life was about to implode or she would not have been included in the meeting. They knew what they saw on the screen was cancer they just didn't know yet what cancer they were dealing with. She explained why the results would take so long and asked me what I would do about work? I didn't understand this question. What could I do? Not go in. And why wouldn't I? She told me I might struggle to concentrate, and at the time I thought it was a ridiculous question, although it's then the seriousness of the situation hit me. Can you work if you have cancer? I stood up to leave, holding a couple of booklets, a lot of questions and 'what if's?' As I left, I realised I had silent 'movie' tears leaking down my face and when I checked my phone, I had so many missed calls from Rob which told him the news he didn't want to hear.

25

The Two Week Wait

The next two-and-a-half weeks were horrendous. We had to wait sixteen days (384 torturous hours if you're counting) to find out the results of the biopsies and scans. I now know that this is because they must process the specimen and then have a planning meeting to discuss the results and decide on treatment. This is all before they see me. I can assure you; this was the hardest part of the entire process.

The 'What ifs?' going around and around in our heads and because we don't have the answers, we filled in the blanks with the help of Dr Google. I should have just gone to a seminar by Dr Nick from the Simpsons. No use telling anyone not to Google, it's human nature but my advice would be to avoid forums and chat rooms. Just as everyone's body is different, so is their diagnosis, treatment and outcome. Trust the specialists and the information online by trusted sources like Cancer Research and Macmillan. Reading about 'breastwarrierJane' from Wigan and her bowel movements, in the wake of her fourth round of treatment, isn't helpful information.

After I returned from my horrendous afternoon at the clinic on that Tuesday, we faced the 'domestic hamster wheel' of family life. When dinner, homework, bed and chores ended, the searching began. I think we both knew. We cried all night. The cycle over the next few weeks, swaying between anger and optimism and hope, clinging onto vaguely remembered sentences from the meeting. The second guessing: did they mean this or that? Having those thoughts swimming around our overcrowded minds was purely exhausting. I knew I couldn't hide it from my colleagues.

We work closely and intensely and; besides, they knew where I was going and why. I had totally played it down because I was genuinely not worried, but that evening, I'd ignored a few texts as I just didn't know what to say.

When I arrived in work, it was obvious things weren't good as Rob and I looked like shit from crying and broken sleep. I told them on mass as I couldn't face saying the same thing over and over, and I didn't want to have to first face them if someone else had told them. It wasn't easy, and I remember saying something like. "We don't know its cancer, but we do really, and I can't hide it, but I don't want to talk about it all day either, and I'm sorry if I'm going to be distracted over the next few weeks, but there it is." It went as expected, and I tried to remain as positive as possible. I didn't want other people to be upset or worried for me.

It seems naïve now, but I couldn't take the responsibility for other people's emotions as mine were demanding and confusing enough. I lasted an hour in work and then left to see the most positive people I know. I needed their take on it as they too had been in this situation. This helped, and I needed that boost. I could go back into work and teach that day, although I don't know how. I tried to keep myself distracted during these weeks, and I also had a few appointments to attend. (Lucky me): a CT scan to see if it had spread anywhere else, bloods, to see whatever that day I had decided where it might have spread, and a heart scan, because the chemo could damage my heart. I had a camera up my bum because I'd been struggling with diarrhoea (pre-lump finding) that photographs and takes samples from the lower bowel. Not painful, but not the most dignified experience of my life. What could be better than seeing tiny stray bits of poo in an otherwise 'spring cleaned' colon-and in HD!

I was so relieved to find out they couldn't see anything nasty but was awaiting biopsy results. I became an expert at flinching and researching every little possible tiny symptom or twinge, trying to put on a brave face in work, continuing to be a good mum. I struggled to be present in any of these situations, as my mind would drift off constantly. I would disappear into my own world, marvelling at the wonders of nature and how lucky I was to wake up to rainfall. Thinking if I did die, should I have a woodland burial or would the ground not fancy my cancer riddled cells leaching into their pure soils. Yep... bloody depressing stuff went through my head during this time. And the minutes felt like hours. Like a child waiting for Christmas or birthdays, the days seemed endless and we've never wanted time to go so quickly. We went to work, we came home, we cooked dinner, we taxied the kids, and we tried to pack up the house, ready for our 'big move'.

We wanted to be a normal couple and family, so we kept a previous arrangement and went to Wales to stay with relatives and decided not to talk about it. We didn't tell them; it was great to escape and walk in the mountains and try not to listen to the kids moaning that it was too far, too cold, they were too wet, as all that didn't matter. Plus, if you paddle in a lake in November, what do you expect? Bloody kids! The weekend was lovely, and we treasured that few days of 'normality' before returning home to worrying, packing and work.

Then, as the week wore on, I got it. Louisa said... what was I going to do about work? This is what she meant. I couldn't play 'Zombie Teacher' much longer, it was making me ill. It was making both of us ill. I wasn't sleeping and felt so run down. I was running on empty. I took a few days off and slept. The house still needed packing up, but we didn't have the energy to do it as we were also playing 'Zombie Parents'. It was very tough time and any spare time we had we were thinking about CANCER. About DYING. Everything that came after this time was all about staying ALIVE!

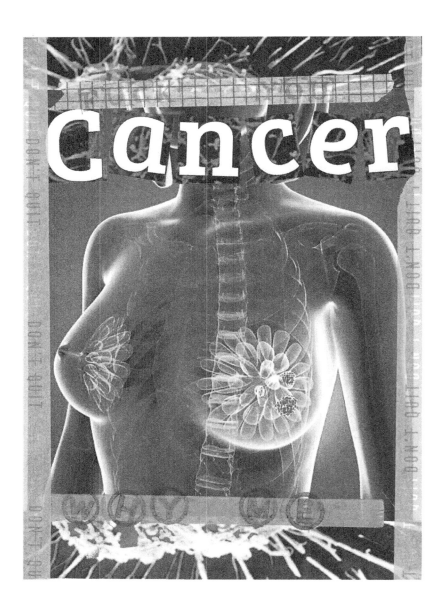

Diagnosis Cancer

Thursday December 7th, 2017. The anticipation of this day had left me feeling really run down. As I'd said, I was struggling to sleep, struggling to work, and the chaos of getting ready to move meant I was frazzled and struggling to function. However, the day arrived, and I couldn't wait to get in there and find out what I was dealing with.

We got the keys to our new house and filled the wardrobes with clothes before leaving for the hospital. I think it was our attempt to take some control back. I knew I had breast cancer. During those sixteen days, so much had changed physically. The lump now felt huge and my nipple was inverting. It was also hot, red and itchy. All the signs and symptoms that I would not have missed. I was just desperate to be reassured it was JUST breast cancer. I couldn't deal with it spreading anywhere, but I knew I had the mental strength to deal with breast cancer.

There was no thunderclap, no lightening moment and no tears. The consultant skirted around the issue until I had to ask rather bluntly, "So is it cancer or not?" I mean, was he not used to this? His actual first words when I sat down were "Oh, don't look at me like that!" I felt like saying, "Look mate, I'm not at the bar waiting to find out what garnish to have in my gin". He was a man in control at that moment and had me eating out of his hand. He was almost jovial, and I couldn't tell if it was making him feel like Donald Trump or he was just a twat. Imagine going to Trump towers for a diagnosis... yep, I know! His approach was to go all round the houses until I heard the word cancer. That's all I was listening for and I remember nothing else he said until I heard that word. CANCER.

It's a dirty word, and it scares the life out of people. But at that point I was so relieved it had spread nowhere other than, as suspected, my lymph nodes. Thank f*** for that! It wasn't; In my bones (they had obviously been aching, and any twinge got me panicking) In my bowels (I'll leave out the toilet talk); In my lungs (obviously the Darth Vader rasping during my last run was because of my poor fitness and an overactive and scared imagination); In my cervix (I was overdue a smear); In my brain (no excuses for being a dizzy cow now and again)

I could go on and on to all the other twinges, aches and things I'd tried not to Google over the last few weeks, but I don't want you to think I'm a total crank. Advice about Dr Google was specifically given again, but did I listen? Do I ever? Really wish I had because it just added to the anxiety and created an unpleasant scenario in my head, mostly around not being here to see the kids grow up. (Oh, and back to my funeral, who would come? How long would it take for my body to decompose?). Delightful thoughts like that again.

I think if my Macmillan nurse had not been in that meeting, I would have left thoroughly confused, but whilst I was just hearing blah, blah, blah, cancer (think Charlie Brown's teacher), she had offered to take notes for me. Maybe she saw my hand trembling as I tried or maybe she knew even though this consultant was speaking English, I couldn't hear anything other than the thoughts of how I'm going to tell my mum, my dad, my kids, echoing in my head. So, Louisa, my Macmillan nurse, had written what I needed to know. And that was it. I was relieved and ready to face this shitty disease head on. I was so glad I had this to refer to over the months as when I'd asked what the difference between grade and stage was; I was met with some strange analogy about a Ford Cortina and a Porsche, to which I'm still perplexed over, and professionally, Louisa seemed keen to wrap up the meeting with the crazy consultant and speak to us on our own. (Maybe she could see 'Diagnosis Murder' on the cards?) I was to see the oncologist the next day as we were all keen to get started on chemo as soon as possible, with Christmas looming and things on the go slow over the festive period. (Soon to be known as the 'worst Christmas' ever). Louisa had the foresight to see I would want to get things in place pretty quickly and I was to find out after my MRI that this tumour was huge and needed shrinking-now!

Officially, the house move was due to happen the next day. But guess what? We left the hospital to news that my buyers' bank had screwed up and the sale couldn't go through until the next week! Grrrrr. Had I been that bad in a former life? It was certainly raining on my parade that day. I didn't care. I let my buyers move in, regardless. I knew and trusted them and couldn't face postponing. Plus, we had virtually packed up the house and had been placed in the same position of trust as purchasers. I had to tell my Mum and Dad, who did not know about what was to come. I was super-strong and super-positive, and probably way too matter of fact. In my head, it would go something like this. *"Hi, I don't want you to worry but I've found a lump, its breast cancer and I'm having chemo then surgery then radiotherapy, but it will all be fine because they do amazing things these days and I'm not worried, so I don't want you to be worried. Okay? Bye"* ...

Actually, it was what wasn't said that was the hardest. It was their expressions and half started questions. But I had this massive urge to protect them, and I didn't want anyone worrying about me. I think I needed everyone to be strong around me so I could be strong. I didn't want to crumble; I didn't want sympathy, and I didn't want to be treated any differently. Part of me is glad I had that attitude, but sometimes I wasn't strong, and I needed to crumble too but didn't feel like I could. It was many months in I realised that's how people saw me anyway and that shocked me. I realised that by putting on a front for all these years people had bought into it and genuinely believed it. I also knew Rob had my back. We would reassure each other, and we could get through this together. Sometimes I think it was harder for him and my family to watch me go through it, than me go through it. I was so lucky as he was my absolute rock.

Grade 2
Lobular Breast Cancer.
ER neg, PR neg Hu 2 positive. *

Doesn't respond to hormones (oestrogen w projesterone)
Herceptin ✓

Advantageous to have Herceptin + Chemotherapy, 80%/response
8/10 cancer reduce in size
2/8 disappear with neo adjuvant chemotherapy

Advice for Breast MRI. Better imaging than mammogram

Neo Adjuvant Chemo – monitor cancer more closely.

Grade 1 – 3   Stage 1 – 4

Cancer cells
down microscope   Ask oncologist

Diagnosis ....
Stage ....
PS 0 1 2 3

Name of Procedure / Treatment Plan (include brief explanation if not clear)

Drugs / Protocol...

No. of cycles................................ Interval between cycles.........................

Blood / Scans / Other tests required ....

Suitable for nurse led clinic (Y) / N

Statement of health professional (to be filled in by health professional with appropriate knowledge of proposed procedure, as specified in consent policy)
I have explained the procedure to the patient/parent (or person who has parental responsibility) In particular, I have explained:

Intended benefits
To reduce the size of the cancer before my operation ☐
To reduce the chance of the cancer coming back after my operation ☐
To cure the cancer ☐
To slow the growth of the cancer ☐
To improve symptoms ☐

Significant, unavoidable or frequently occurring risks:

☐ Increased risk of infection
☐ Anaemia and increased risk of bleeding
☐ Nausea and vomiting
☐ Hair loss
☐ Tiredness
☐ Loss of taste
☐ Mouth ulcers
☐ Difficulty Swallowing
☐ Difficulty Breathing
☐ Allergic reactions
☐ Skin rash / reaction
☐ Diarrhoea
☐ Constipation
☐ Urinary Problems
☐ Hearing loss
☐ Painful hands and feet
☐ Numbness and tingling in hands and feet
☐ Muscle aches and pains
☐ Heart problems
☐ Premature menopause
☐ Osteoporosis
☐ Infertility
☐ Other (please specify)

Toxicity of chemotherapy can be life threatening

Top copy accepted by patient Yes / No (Please Circle)

3

The Morning after the Day Before

F**king hell... I have got breast cancer!!! All the feelings of fear and bewilderment lasted a few seconds before I realised; I need to live by the motto I preach to the kids I work with. "You can't change what happens to you, but you can change how you deal with it". Oh balls! Why did I have to be so positive?

I had slept a little. I'd got up about midnight and started packing the kitchen stuff as I needed to be distracted, and it gave me a good few hours to think and despair over how much I had yet to do to enable our house move. I had to push the negatives away because I couldn't even go there; it was too scary. It was much easier to be positive. At that point I thought-I have got this. It hasn't spread further than the lymph nodes, and I trust these doctors. I'm not afraid of breast cancer, I can deal with it. I didn't allow myself to think any other way. I didn't feel sorry for myself and I don't think I really cried. Looking back, I was numb and too busy to worry. I found this inner strength I didn't know I had and just got on with it. Cancer isn't in charge, I am! F**k you cancer. And f**k you packing (It's overrated, isn't it!)

I don't know how I emptied the house that day, but it happened, and I did it before seeing an oncologist at 4pm. I was gross by then. I didn't realise she was going to examine my 'sweaty mess': cobwebs in my hair, and my body covered in dust and grime. Thankfully, she was lovely, and I remember actually cracking a few jokes. It was good for my mum (who had only had twenty-four hours to process this damn cancer news), as we were reassured that they can cure it and rid me of this bastard. However, there was a catch, (why is there always a catch?) to get rid of the nasty cells they will also have to kill the good cells too, and apart from the obvious loss of hair associated with chemo, I had to sign to say I understood that this will feel like it's killing me before it cures me. Ok, so not quite put like that, but it is essentially what is meant.

Check out the list of side effects and take the ticks as a given. I had bloody all of these, and then some. Of course, knowing this would have changed nothing. I wanted it gone, and that is the price you have to pay if you choose chemo. It was my choice. I could have said no and brewed some wild plants whilst eating rabbit food, in the hope of a cure. Ha! I was way too scared for that 'hippy shit', even if it has worked for some. So, the decision was made. I was booked in for the 20th of December for my first chemotherapy treatment. Happy Christmas to me! The most expensive Christmas present ever was coming my way, courtesy of the NHS.

Sharing the Good News

How the hell do you tell people you have cancer? Well, social media, private messaging helps, so I sent out a few group messages that went something like this....

Ok guys, not so great news this time. Would you believe I've just been diagnosed with breast cancer? It's treatable, and the aim is to cure it, and I start chemo next week. I've been wanting to message before now but haven't had a minute because as well as that, we have just moved to a new house, so life is manic!! Finished work last week, as I can't get my head around work/move/xmas/cancer! Rob is being amazing, but I worry about the toll on him. Feel really lucky it hasn't spread and that the medicine combination is so good these days. I hope you all have better news!!! Love to you all xxx.

That was easy. Commit a few matter-of-fact words into the screen and be as positive as possible. What was the hardest thing I have ever had to do was tell the kids, especially my daughter, who had already been through so much change at 10 years old and was vulnerable. As expected, she was distraught. I was very honest but my response to, "Are you going to die?" was, "Yes, when I'm ninety odd and smelling of cabbage". I don't think she laughed. I never believed it would kill me, as I just would not allow it to take my life and believed I had that much control over it.

Mya was very clingy that night and cried herself to sleep in my arms, clinging on like a baby monkey, until she star-fished me out of her bed.

My stepson's dealt with it privately, but can you imagine how weird it must have been for them? I'd been in their life a relatively short time and they didn't really know me all that well, and yet this news would throw them too. Jonny was quietly protective but privately angry at the situation. Ben didn't say much but what could he say? Initially, the crazy three-year-old was none the wiser other than me having a sore boob, and as the months wore on, no hair. Yet it was more loss and change for him in his already brief life.

Looking back, I didn't prepare and support them as I could have but maybe that's the point; I couldn't because I was processing it all myself. I was also feeling dreadful. A few days later I was diagnosed with acute tonsillitis and was prescribed antibiotics and flu jab combo. Also, I was still physically exhausted and probably quite traumatised by the diagnosis.

Before chemo was to start on the 20th, I still had to work, visit the Lilac Centre (a satellite for Clatterbridge and a 'chemo haven') and visit the wig-man to sort a new 'do' in the event of me losing mine. We were also unpacking, changing addresses, buying and wrapping Christmas presents, sorting bills, and beginning renovations for our new house and oh.... did I mention the wedding?

This was the weekend we decided to bring the wedding forward. Never ones to shy away from a challenge, and in the event of this stupid bloody cancer, our plan for a small summer 2018 wedding went out of the window once the diagnosis had sunk in. I wasn't expecting to pop my clogs, but I didn't know how frail, bald, sick, fat or tired I'd be, and we liked the idea of a distraction and focusing on a positive- anything other than cancer! Anyway, three weeks is enough time to organise a wedding, isn't it? Over Christmas AND New Year?

We did it with (wedding) bells on. Focusing on the important bits like a licence, venue, attire, rings, grub and invites by text... it was sorted. Thank God for online shopping. Family took charge of suits for the boys and bridesmaid dresses for the girls. Friends organised and gifted me my flowers and make up. My hair (well, my wig) was booked in for that morning and that was all we needed. We were genuinely excited for this new adventure awaiting us.

Until then we still had work, chemo, Christmas and New Year to contend with. I was intending to work until I had to start chemo, as this would take me to the Christmas holidays and so I could start my sick leave officially in the January. However, after my official diagnosis and moving day, I went into work and just couldn't concentrate. I didn't have the headspace to think about teaching and assessment, never mind the mental health support I wanted to give the students in my care. It didn't feel fair to be popping in and out for appointments as they needed consistency. Plus-I just didn't have it in me. So, I bit the bullet and told all the kids after break time that I was leaving to be treated for breast cancer. It didn't feel right to leave it to anyone else. No one said much, and I picked up my bag and I left. Just like that. Rob (my soon to be husband) went upstairs to his office and cried. I didn't even think how hard that was for him; I was just trying to be strong and not cry myself.

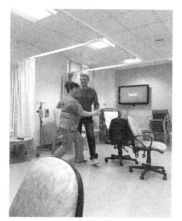

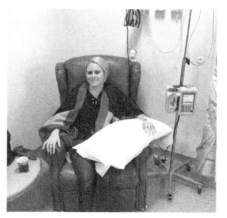

Chemotherapy One

Chemo side effects are not something I ever want to experience again, but I remember desperately wanting to start it and just get it over with. I hadn't slept all night. Not because of nerves or excitement, but because of the steroids that were preparing my body for the onslaught of these awful drugs and making me hyper. I wasn't scared to start this treatment; I was pleased to be getting the hell on with it. My breast was definitely getting bigger, more painful, and my nipple was inverting by the hour. (Well, not quite, but it adds to the visual image).

I was due in at 9am and after a brief wait, they introduced me to the nurse who would administer my first drug by hand. Before they put anything in or near you, they have to follow protocol and ask you many questions about your health and to check with every drug, that you are who you say you are. I'd had blood tests two days previously so they could see if I was medically fit enough to accept the chemicals, with no damage occurring, and I was ready. It only took just over an hour and I felt fine. Everyone had been so supportive and lovely, and Rob even had a Christmas waltz with one nurse.

The staff have a fine balance of professional and personal qualities, to put you at ease and help you relax, making the experience as comfortable and less intimidating as possible. Difficult when they are administering thousands of pounds' worth of toxic medicine into your bloodstream.

One drug is bright red and has to be administered by hand-if not, you will explode! I'm joking, but it can burn your tissue if it comes out of your veins, and thankfully, it never did, but it burned slightly within the vein.

I felt a bit of a fraud when I left as if nothing had happened and still felt wired. I was probably running on a mixture of adrenaline and more steroids, as I felt pretty good. On the way home, we called into my mum's and she made us bacon butties, which tasted divine and was a bit of respite from playing the side effect waiting game. As we were both aware, I was a ticking time bomb.

I felt tired later that first day and nauseous, but I wondered if I was imagining it or if it was real. I hadn't been a picture of health to start with and felt exhausted from lack of sleep and adrenaline of the morning but buzzing from the steroids. I decided it was like that strange feeling of being drunk from your first ever dalliance with alcohol, but if I'm honest, it wasn't awful, just very surreal.

The next day it was like being a fly on the wall; watching myself go through the motions and feeling like nothing I have ever experienced. However, whilst I convinced myself I could smash this, I knew the worst could be yet to come. And boy was I right.

That Friday brought my first day of no steroids, but the first of seven injections called Filgrastim. This little beauty stimulates white blood cells so your body fights infection. Sounds great, doesn't it? Chemo kills the cells which help maintain your white blood count. Filgrastim jabbed in my belly, stimulated my body to produce more white blood cells. It left me feeling fluey and achy, like I was fighting an infection. Every morning in my belly fat... boom! 'There you go'. A little vial of aches and pains in your bones and joints.

That afternoon I got a call from my oncologist to tell me the results from the heart scan I'd had a few weeks before. It revealed my chemo needed to change to a different regimen, and I had to take blood pressure tablets for the foreseeable future, as a precaution and to avoid damage to my poor little heart. Wonderful news, this just gets better. However, it wasn't all bad. I was also lucky enough to be prescribed Dom Perignon, or at least that's what we called the anti-sickness drug, Domperidone. In all honesty, it was a token gift and didn't really touch the sides. It was like having a cider ice lolly and waiting to get drunk.

If you're reading this and going through treatment, don't wait until cycle three to ask for more drugs. They have a big range of alternatives and do not want anyone to suffer, and they are happy to dish them out. I was just a martyr and thought everyone felt like this. I felt I had to get on with it at first. You could say I learnt the hard way. Also, I've never enjoyed taking tablets, which was ironic, don't you think? Thankfully, you are not left alone and can contact the hospital to ask for advice, or just check in. These people really are wonderful saviours who will do what they can to make your experience as manageable as it can be. I just had to learn to ask.

Not So 'Merry Christmas'

On Christmas Eve, four days post chemo, I decided that this was the day to venture out of the house because I felt like a cooped-up, sick chicken. Rob didn't want me to go, but I knew better, of course! I wish I'd listened. I've never driven whilst drunk but by then I felt too out of it to realise how dangerous it was for me to be driving and it never occurred to me, until I was driving home, that I really shouldn't have been on the road. I thought I'd be better for getting out.

The trip to the shops didn't last long. I felt like I had a big sign over my head saying, 'please avoid and excuse, I've had chemo!' I was burning up, felt dizzy, like I was an alien going shopping for the first time. Like a doddery version of Daryl Hannah in Splash when she escapes to the shopping mall. (Obviously I was wearing clothes, it was December after all). I cried when I got home and collapsed into a deflated heap onto the sofa. It was Christmas, a time of fun, family and festivities, and I couldn't even handle an aisle in Pound Stretcher.

After a 'nana nap', I felt better and enjoyed a delicious steak with rosemary potatoes and roasted vegetables. I even managed a tiny Bucks Fizz and felt smug, thinking, 'this Chemo lark isn't too bad after all'. Little did I know, it wouldn't be the last time I saw the contents of my plate. A few nights previously, Rob had gone out at 10pm to buy another electronic thermometer, as we were paranoid about not being able to detect an infection. We were under strict instructions to go straight to

A&E if I developed a temperature above 37. 5 °, as this could be a sign of an infection or sepsis. I went to bed early that Christmas Eve, as I was zapped of all energy and enthusiasm by this point. My temp was fine, according to the three thermometers I was then checking neurotically. We were expecting an early wake-up call from the kids (they had been on the good list after all) so I just wanted to get some sleep in the hope I felt ok on Christmas Day, for their sake.

Two hours later, I was dreaming of being pulled out of a river and woke up feeling drenched and freezing. I felt sick, shivery, and like I'd not slept for a week. Typically, my temp was up on all three thermometers, so I woke up a snoring Rob, drafted in my mum and dad to drive over and look after the now sleeping kids, and we set out for the first trip to A&E. Merry Christmas to us!

A chemo card (when the staff at the A and E reception know what one is) is gold dust to a chemo patient as it scares the life out of the medical staff, and they jump. They do not allow you to sit in hospital or doctor's waiting rooms when receiving active treatment because of the risk of infection. If you are well, this is brilliant, as it feels like a perk. (Imagine getting excited about not queuing for blood tests or sitting with everyone else in a waiting room). If you are sick, you don't care where you are sitting, you just want to feel vaguely human again. It was Christmas Day by about five minutes when I got to triage, having been isolated whilst I waited. They actually asked me to leave that area to make way for a cancer patient having active treatment and who was therefore vulnerable. I had to explain as I was slumped in a wheelchair, fifty shades of grey, that the patient was me.

The next few hours, I had a series of blood tests and an ECG. They treated me as if I had sepsis and I was given fluids and IV antibiotics. It was only when I was wheeled through for a chest X-ray, I unleashed holy hell on the poor x-ray guy. Three paper kidney trays of steak dinner puke and a side of slimy mushrooms and asparagus. But DAMN, did I feel better after this! Not sure it was the river of puke or the IV Cyclizine that was administered shortly afterwards, but life suddenly became more bearable. Rob tells me at that point it's because I was off my face; the nurse told me this is the 'bag heads' drug of choice when they can't score. I didn't care. It felt like a miracle. I've obviously never used Heroin, but Cyclizine is pretty good stuff, even though it stings like hell if they administer it too fast.

Eventually, after a wee sample to check I've not got a urine infection, (which sat in the room for two hours and could well still be there,) we could leave and drive back to Christmas. It was 4 am, and we hoped Santa had; a–visited; b–rewound all the clocks and c–drugged the kids so they didn't think us stumbling in is indeed, the Man in Red. We found my mum and dad curled up on the sofa. (I think maybe my dad ate the minced pie and drank Santa's whiskey). We sent them on their way, happy that I was home and that they could go to bed.

One hour's sleep later and we were propped in front of the Christmas tree with four excited kids and gutted we didn't feel the same. I hadn't expected that Santa bringing the crazy three-year-old a speaker with attached disco light would bring me such misery. I felt like I was dying and didn't much appreciate the irony of 'In my mind, in my head by Dynoro and Gigi D'agostino' on repeat, accompanied by a disco ball strobe, targeting my fragile brain. Hangovers and kids don't mix and

48

neither does chemo and kids, especially when they act like they have eaten a lifetime supply of Haribo.

Somehow, we opened presents, ate breakfast (I demolished some breadsticks) and we went to Manchester to have our family Christmas dinner. I do not know how we got through this day (maybe it was the drugs) but we did, and I was so glad when it was over. You'll be thrilled to know the rest of Christmas was uneventful, which is just how I liked it, and each day, I slowly returned from the 'upside down' to myself.

I had my first MRI the following week which I'd been dreading and was insisting I'd need sedatives to get into the machine. It isn't pleasant to be manoeuvred into a narrow, million-pound smartie tube, but I went in feet first and lying on my front, which took some claustrophobia away. Even though it was so noisy (think being strapped to a jumbo jet whilst it's landing) and uncomfortable, it was somewhat bearable.

I was super proud of myself for getting through it, and yet for the first time I could do nothing but reflect on the past few weeks and think about what we had all been through so far. I couldn't believe I was in this situation. I became cross with myself that I'd not been more vigilant in checking for lumps or changes, as I'd thought I was good at it. I clearly hadn't done for months and knew this was something that I wanted to educate people on. I just didn't know how at that point. How could I have missed something so big? It felt ridiculous, like when you hear about someone giving birth but without knowing they were ever pregnant. Alas, this was the situation I had found myself in and I guess I had to be thankful I'd found it when I did, as those few months probably saved my life.

 **Firstofthemonthcheckforalump**
3 January 2018 · 🌐

So 2017 was eventful. Ran a marathon, got divorced, moved house, got engaged, ran four half marathons, got diagnosed with breast cancer. Weirdly I've never been happier. I feel very positive I can kick cancers arse and have lots of support. Many people have been asking is there anything they can do for me and yes there is. Please on the first of every month, check for a lump. Using this date should be a great reminder that we need to check for lumps regularly. I'm sure some of you already do if you don't then start now. It takes minutes and could save your life. When you have then you can like this post or comment done. Thanks for all your support so far, but please do this for yourselves as well as me. This is me having chemo on the 20th. Chemo is a bitch! She is not to be messed with and brought me misery Day 4- 9 post infusion. BUT I'm thinking of the long game and that she is being cruel to be kind! So go and check your boobs and balls and remember #firstofthemonthcheckforalump (please share this too)

👍❤️😮 Nicola Pope and 29 others   3 comments 27 shares

👍 Like   💬 Comment   ↪ Share

3,630 people reached ❯   [Boost Post]

 Firstofthemonthcheckforalump updated their cover photo.
3 January 2018 · 🌐

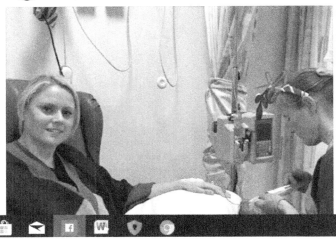

50

First of the Month Check for a Lump

I felt so silly when asked how I found my lump, mainly because I had to explain why I'd missed such an enormous mass in my breast. I felt foolish and really bloody annoyed with myself for a good while. I've previously mentioned I thought I was good at checking. Clearly not. The MRI had confirmed the mass was a huge 7cm by 9cm, and this was after my first round of chemo. How had I missed a small orange playing hide and seek in my boob? I'd had fibroadenoma's diagnosed in the past, so I'd thought checking had become second nature. Since diagnosis I'd done a lot of googling and learned you should check your boobs at least once a month for lumps and be vigilant for visual changes too.

Having had lots of time to think (I know... such a lazy arse at this point) over the past few weeks, I came up with the tagline #firstofthemonthcheckforalump. At that point, I wasn't planning a campaign. If I could inform friends and family 'on mass' of my cancer progress through Facebook, I could also remind them to check every month too. To be honest, initially I had no intention of ever talking about cancer on Facebook, but I was outed by someone wishing me luck on my newsfeed who had heard from a friend. This then prompted a lot of concerned messages. I certainly didn't want any sympathy 'likes' or attention seeking posts resulting in 'PM me now hon' comments. That's not me. What happened was quite organic. I realised I could use my negative, shitty situation and turn it into a positive by helping to raise awareness and update friends and family. This, without having to answer a trillion texts or emails with the same boring responses, (from me not them, I appreciated every single message that came my way and still do). It's a fine line, isn't it? But the messages of thanks I received certainly made it worthwhile to sell my soul to the 'Facebook Devil'. People I knew, and some I didn't, thanked me, as it had prompted an anxious time waiting to be checked. Some found early cancers, some found nothing more than reassurance, thankfully. A good friend went to get a lump in his testicle checked and within the month was receiving treatment and had surgery for testicular cancer. He said he wouldn't have addressed it without my prompts. So effectively, I'd saved his life whilst I had an army of people trying to save mine..

Firstofthemonthcheckforalump
3 January 2018 · 🌐

Thanks for following. I'm pleased to say that I've had two people private message me to say my post prompted them to check and they have booked appointments to see a doctor because they have found lumps. Hopefully they will be given the all clear 👍 and I wish them well xx

👍❤️ Lauren Hill and 81 others

👍 Like   💬 Comment   ↪ Share

822 people reached ❯

Boost Post

Hair today: Gone Tomorrow

Thursday Jan 4th, 2018. 15 days Post chemo

It was two days before my wedding, and I'd had a dilemma: my hair was desperate for a wash and I'd been putting it off so I could try to keep it for the wedding, but I knew deep down it was unlikely.

For days now it had been coming out all over the house, by the handful. I was that paranoid about its fragility, I'd held it to my head on the way from the car to the hospital the previous day as it was so windy, and I literally thought it was going to blow off my scalp 'cartoon style'. To many, losing your hair is the most traumatic element of chemotherapy. Personally, I think it's much easier to lose it than the stages of it growing back and all the issues that may bring. But I understand that losing hair (everywhere) has a real impact on self-image and confidence. Especially if you lose your brows and lashes.

After trying to give it a good brush and insulting it with dry shampoo, I knew I needed to bite the bullet and 'wash and go' for it. I had to laugh at the trauma at the bottom of the shower tray, but that was nothing of the bird's nest that was now on top of my head. I fought back the tears and laughed as I attempted to brush the disaster that was now my hair. It was impossible, and there was only one thing left for it.

I hacked away until a badly mowed lawn of tufty grey and brown remained; I was in the house alone and surrounded by hair, wondering if Rob's beard trimmer could finish the job and realising; I had little choice as I was too embarrassed to go anywhere looking like I did. Looking back, I'm sure a hairdresser would have taken pity on me and helped me out, but I'm stupidly proud and didn't want to ask.

Fortunately, the clippers worked, and I only had a bit to finish when they ran out of power (not fair!) I embraced my fresh look and threw some make up on distracting from my shaved head. I took some selfies of my efforts to send to Rob, who obviously gave me full approval. I really could have done with him there to help, but I think deep down it was almost a 'rite of cancer passage' I needed to go down alone. I threw 'Britney' (my new wig) on over the top and faced the world. My mum and daughter did not want to see. In fact, it freaked them out for some time, and I know both found it hard to see me bald for a while as losing hair through chemotherapy is such a physical symbol of cancer and one they did not want to face. Who does? But this was now reality, and I needed acceptance.

I'd had the choice to wear a cold cap but was always someone who hated feeling cold, so it just wasn't an option. Also, I wasn't too impressed as it wasn't a guarantee of retaining the entire head of hair. It was hard enough to sit and endure chemo, never mind feeling like your head is covered in a hat of ice-pops. I understand it's a personal choice and hats off to anyone who can be bothered to go through that (or hats on!) but it wasn't for me, so a 'baldy' I was to be. For now.

56

Going to the Town Hall and we're gonna get ma-a-a-ried

The preparations had been straightforward. We had to meet with the registrar and apply for a special licence and whilst they were compassionate and supportive; it was a very formal and scary process. It made my diagnosis so real as I had to request a letter from the consultant, proving I had breast cancer!

Before starting my treatment, my breast cancer nurse Louisa had got me an appointment with the 'Wig man' Shaun. She knew that with Christmas and the impending holidays, we needed to act fast, in case I lost my hair before the wedding. I had been excited about this process and was made to feel at ease from the off. Who knew there would be a room in the clinic that acted as a mock salon? And that an experienced hairdresser worked to provide you a glimmer of femininity and dignity, whilst going through your treatment?

I chose my wig, not really understanding who pays for it, but I think its charity money and I was incredibly grateful. Get this! As you know my wig was called 'Britney' and it was fabulous. Long, luscious layers. and exactly the opposite of my hair. I had wanted long hair since as a child, watching Jim'll Fix It... (Bear with me on this), when the girls received their badge with the thick red ribbon draped over their head, they would lift their trapped long hair and flick it out over the top. I thought this was just ace! How shallow… Thank God I never wrote in!

So, back to the wedding. We now needed to find a suitable venue for an afternoon wedding breakfast for 150 friends and family. There was only one option really, and with Rob pulling in a favour, we booked one of the function rooms at the rugby stadium. It was a hot buffet with basic table decorations. We didn't have the inclination or the money for any fuss or colour schemes. It was to be a no frills wedding and about us celebrating and sharing our day with friends and family.

I only wish we had forked out for a professional photographer. Not to undermine the great work that our two ex-students did with the pictures they took, and it was lovely to have them part of our day, but I still, to this day, haven't organised and edited them to create an album and I regret that. We were lucky enough to have another ex-student, a singer, to provide our entertainment. A friend had organised a treat and craft table for the kids and the entire day felt natural and laid back, just what we had intended.

There were obviously a few people who wondered what the hell we were doing. No-one dared question us, but I could see pity in a few eyes that day, but I didn't let it phase me. We knew we were getting married because of love, not because of cancer. That had just given us the kick up the arse to get on with it and have a big party. I could also see raw emotion in some of our guests' eyes, as it really was a beautiful day and ceremony. I didn't think I'd make it down the aisle without sobbing, but we had to drag the crazy three-year-old, who refused to walk with me. Myself and my Dad had to lift him, and his little legs were in mid-air which broke the ice and made everyone laugh. I look back and cringe at the state of him. His little blue suit was drowning him, and his boots are still too big to this day, poor boy, good job he is cute. He had been fascinated by my baldy head and lack of hair but when he saw me with my wig on and in my wedding dress for the first time that day he said, "You look pretty, Mummy, but where has your fallen out hair gone?"

I melted when I saw Rob and I know its soppy, but it was truly a magical moment. That day I was just Sarah, not Sarah with cancer. One round of chemo and a lot of drugs in... that felt amazing. I was even brave enough by the end of the wedding party to throw my hair (wig) off and dance like I didn't have a care in the world. It was hot and sweaty, and I wore it in the end for other people, not myself!

I've had a lot of comments since, that people have fond memories of that day and the staff there, who were amazing, said it was one of the nicest weddings they have worked. I even did a speech, which was totally unplanned. I felt it was important to thank everyone personally for coming to help us celebrate, and so I waffled on for a bit and got a few laughs. I was buzzing from the steroids, so maybe it was just one laugh, as I'm no Victoria Wood. By the time we got home at 6pm and ordered a take-away, I was bloody shattered. There is a photo of our romantic wedding evening where we are toasting our day in PJ's with freshly plastered walls in the background whilst we ate our curry! It makes me smile as that day made me a thrilled Mrs Vaughan.

Firstofthemonthcheckforalump

7 January 2018 · 🌐

· · ·

So I'm feeling brave after my wonderful wedding yesterday. Unfortunately, my hair didn't make the guest list as it was coming out in handfuls. I shaved it off after hacking it away with scissors (by then it was a tatty ball on my head anyway) this was Thursday so I had a few days to get used to wearing my wig before the big day. I took this picture before I put 'Brittany' (the name of my wig 😜) on before going to the ceremony. I felt empowered and wanted to share with you. I don't miss my hair but my head is cold, it's like going outside in the winter with wet hair. I'll be experimenting with headwear but you'll also see me bald and proud. **#nohairdontcare**

👍❤️ Rebecca Twist and 321 others

112 comments 8 shares

👍 Like   💬 Comment   ↪ Share

7,616 people reached >

Boost Post

61

January Blues

Day three of married life and Rob went back to work, and I went for my pre-chemo bloods. 'Rock and flippin roll'.

I really felt it that day, the realisation that I couldn't go back to normal life and this was my new normal for now. I was living in a house that didn't feel like home yet, and the builders were back for a good few months of renovation chaos. 60 Minute Makeover it was not. We had to put our stamp on it and to make it feel like 'our house'. This included converting the loft, the garage, the utility and stripping and plastering most of the house. Probably not the best timing, but it was a very good, if not messy, distraction.

But waking up that day was scary. I wasn't in control, about to start the steroids and dreading Wednesday's second round of chemo. I was hyped for the first chemo, but that day I felt lonely and scared. I was effectively off sick but waiting to feel really sick and we had months like this. I felt isolated and worried about what was to come, but I had no choice but to crack on and get on with it or crack up.

I got to the Lilac Centre to find my drugs hadn't yet arrived. My dealer was still asleep, and I couldn't score! They were in a taxi on their way as there had been a cock up with the drugs having to change, because of the heart issue. All I know it was a long day. I think we were one of the last to leave and I was, despite the steroids, exhausted. That evening the exhaustion turned to despair, I had a backlash from a family member about some pictures I had posted on Facebook of me whilst having chemo. They offended her and she demanded I take them down. I refused. I was using humour to get through this and felt strongly that whilst I knew how serious chemo was and is; I wanted to take the mystery away by letting people know I was ok and being brave, then they could brave for me. Or something like that.

Now I understand it was torture for family to see me going through this. And it had hit her hard. I now know she felt out of control and scared, but what followed was really hard to deal with. I went through the next few days with no contact from her, and I was feeling debilitated from the chemo and the snotty cold I had picked up from somewhere. These were some of my darkest hours, and those January days were most certainly blue.

The reason for including this story is not to bad mouth this person (who really is the kindest person I know) but to convey that whilst the person with cancer is suffering physically and mentally, so are their family and friends and they don't always please us with how they deal with it. Here, she was clearly coming to terms with my diagnosis and hurting. As I think was I.

In my experience it is also very much a flight, fight, freeze response for anyone in our lives how they react. Cancer is very scary, and I imagine many people hear C word and visualise death. But I wasn't ready to pop my clogs yet.

To 'pop' – is slang for taking something to a pawnbroker. If you are pawning clogs, one would assume the person is who wore them is now deceased. Hence the term!

It must be awful to watch those you love going through such a traumatic time, and there is no handbook how to cope with it. However, when I reflect on who in my life wasn't particularly supportive during this time, I don't feel anger or malice. I don't feel those friends who didn't reach out are bad people, I just think they couldn't handle it. Previously, I'm not sure I've always been there for people when they have needed me and have worried, I may say or do the wrong thing. In the future, I'd like to think this would help people to understand that you just need to communicate how you feel. Write a message that says I really want to help, but I'm not sure how and don't want to disturb you or don't know what you might need. Or just be brave and guess. I bet you can't get it wrong.

I had lost a friend who had died from cancer and spent weeks wondering if I should make her some soups or juices to help with the effects of her treatment, as I knew she was having problems with her digestion. Those weeks I spent pondering, I should have just done it and left them on the doorstep with a note through the door. What did I have to lose? It was silly that I worried if it was the right thing to do and then did nothing. I've never forgotten that or forgiven myself. But I also realise this may have happened with me. Maybe I was being thought about by those friends who didn't step up, but they just didn't know what to do for the best.

Of course, there are many types of friendship, and unfortunately when you need support from those friends who you think you can rely on, you realise some friendships are based on short-term gain. You may have those friends who you always party with, or your gym buddy whom you feel close to, until it comes to support. It's like a kick in the teeth when they aren't there for you, because your perception of your relationship is that you shared more than drinking or exercising. Your expectations of these friendships may only be challenged when you're in need. In my experience, this can be why people surprise us in situations where we want and need their friendship, but they don't always come up with the goods. You realise those relationships and friendships were actually superficial, and this can hurt.

I wasn't bitter because it was also much nicer to concentrate on the messages of support, notes and thoughtful gifts I received. Someone lovely turned up one day with Manuka honey and bottled water... simple but so thoughtful and welcomed. I had meals brought round, which was a godsend. A friend who came to see me regularly even tidied my crazy three-year-old's bedroom, and I had friends who picked up the kids and looked after them, often taking them out for tea. A lifelong school friend, whom I rarely see these days, messaged me on the morning of every chemo to wish me luck. Another friend would drive from Lytham to bring me lunch. I received lovely care packages, bamboo socks, flowers, superwoman biscuits, pink ribbon running leggings, cards and amazing, thoughtful words and I much preferred to concentrate on those.

I must mention Rhona, my friend who worked long hours and got little time off. She would visit to give me company and rightly so, tell me off for not bothering with the shower or forgetting (sometimes on purpose) to take my meds. She even fed me after my surgery as I was so weak. She is one tough cookie and through many hours of kindness, also told me to "suck it up and get on with it" when I was really contemplating not finishing the chemo. It was really refreshing to have that honesty.

I'm truly thankful for every single ounce of support I received, and it kept me going during those dark days. Although January was a tough month I didn't want to repeat, I was very lucky I had so much good in my life.

Firstofthemonthcheckforalump

Chemo number 2!! All good so far apart from steroids keeping me awake all night! Remind me to save some for when I'm well enough for gin nights out! 😊

OO Rebecca Twist and 123 others   32 comments

👍 Like   💬 Comment   ↪ Share

Boost Post

Firstofthemonthcheckforalump
10 January 2018

All done 🎤 singing 'I will survive' on smooth in the car! Some picture to make you smile

😀😮😍 Rhona Westhead and 85 others   5 comments

👍 Like   💬 Comment   ↪ Share

Boost Post

Finding Chemo

Think chemo and the image of the poorly baldy patient sat hooked up to IV drugs springs to mind, doesn't it? Admit it...it fills you with dread and you hope never to be in that situation. If you've been there, you hope to never be in that vulnerable situation again, don't you?

But chemotherapy saves lives. The research for many cancers is very advanced, which means the outcome for lots of us is positive. This in a nutshell means I won't die. Well, I will but hopefully I'll be ninety-eight and smelling of trumps by then, won't I Mya? However, what I didn't realise is that in trying to cure me it was going to kill me first. Well, that's what it felt like, slowly and painfully.

Chemotherapy treatment is vast. Some people have it every day or every week for a set length of time, other people have it every three weeks, including myself. I naively thought chemotherapy was the name of a drug that killed cancer cells. Until chemo arrived at my door, I didn't know that it can be taken orally at home, and in hospital or cancer centre, and intravenously. The cycles can go on for weeks, months or years, and the combinations of drugs can vary from single drug doses to many during one cycle. I was prescribed a regimen that included three cycles of FEC, then Docetaxel and Trastuzumab (Herceptin) and Pertuzumab. This would be six cycles, every three weeks, taking five months to complete. If my body was willing. I knew my head was, as I desperately wanted to smash breast cancer out of the water.

How apt that my regimen was called FEC. Yeah, FEC off cancer! FEC stands for:

F-fluorouracil. Apparently one of the most common drugs to treat cancer and known as 5FU (I can see a pattern here). The list of potential side effects is endless, and I wouldn't read about it in too much detail. If you are reading this because you are about to start it, then don't, unless its medical information provided by your team. Dr Google isn't nice, and everyone's body reacts differently to what we put in it. We all want help and hope but leave it to the experts!

E-epirubicin involves bright red liquid being hand pumped into your veins through a cannula, with the nurse staring at your veins for the duration. This is to check it doesn't leak out as it can permanently damage your tissue. Pain free at the time (if stingy) but it aggravated my veins, and it was painful for months after. Is also makes your wee bright red, but that was quite funny. The three-year-old wondered why I'd put blackcurrant Claudia (cordial) down the loo.

C-cyclophosphamide increases the risk of premature menopause (an advantage for some) and can be a carcinogenic! I trusted the benefits outweighed the risks. Also, another list longer than my arm of side effects. But these oncologists have done their homework, and I believe they know what they are doing. But get this... the consent forms list death as a risk factor!

So, the side effects...

Who says the effects of chemo are grim? They're not grim. They are a 'grim sandwich' between 'two slices of grim', with 'grim on the side'.

It's not like that for everyone. Obviously, there are so many types of chemotherapy and our bodies respond in unexpected ways, so when you receive the information on the list of side effects, it's a lottery which you will get. (Something to look forward to, at least). I'm not sure I really understood that it could be a tick list and that by the end of the chemotherapy stint, I think I ticked all the boxes and more. I know at this point I am moaning. I mean, of course, there are people worse off but chemo was brutal, and I make no apologies for the next chapter which is depressing because that was my experience and I think it's important to be honest. So here goes:

I knew that chemotherapy could make you feel sick, but I want you to think of the worst hangover, with the worst flu, while feeling you are still drunk. So, if you can take yourselves there, then you may have some idea what it's like.

Fortunately, the brilliant oncologists are very keen to prescribe anti-sickness drugs to counteract these side effects. Unfortunately for me, they didn't work that well and as each cycle progressed with cumulative effects; they put me on stronger and stronger meds.

I had an impressive collection of anti-sickness tablets by the end of my treatment and had it down to a fine art - what I could take and when. Or so I thought. I realised I hadn't listened, processed or read the advice properly and would double-up on two of the medications. When I told the nurse, she was horrified because the side effects of mixing the drugs were chronic constipation. Constipation sounded like bliss compared with the code brown full-flow I had been experiencing. My bum was so sore from the constant explosive diarrhoea and I'm sure shares in Andrex had risen sharply that spring. What I was saving in shampoo was being ploughed back into loo roll, without question. Also, not great, is as mentioned, I was sharing the loo with several builders and it was impossible to be discreet.

In my head I needed that combination of anti-sickness because it was just so dreadful feeling so poorly and I desperately wanted to take control back. Looking back, it was a really silly thing to think that I could manage my medication, when I could barely walk to get a drink.

Back to puking up. I felt constantly sick and trying to take these meds and my steroids without throwing up became the focus of my day.

Typically, the steroids were cheeky little blighters that got stuck in my throat frequently and they tasted disgusting. I can still remember that taste now, and it makes me heave. So, the times they would get stuck in my throat (which was already sore and blistered) and I would then be sick, and the steroid would still be stuck, so then I would not only still be tasting the steroid, but I'd also be trying not to be sick and having to drink to swallow it down, whilst crying (again). It just felt like another bit of torture.

During the last few cycles, I would sit for hours (or maybe it was minutes but felt like hours) trying to pluck up the courage to take these medicines without being sick. It was then when I came up with the plan. I would imagine that Brad Pitt was sitting next to me on the sofa. Who wants to throw up in front of Brad Pitt? I bet that won't impress him much. I would swallow them with the safety net of the sick bowl on my lap, trying to focus on watching 'Homes Under the Hammer', with Brad and not focus on the vomit that was ascending. I was so pleased with myself if I could do it, and I'd like to say I had it down to a fine art in the end, but actually I caved in and asked for liquid steroids.

Another beautiful side effect was the nasal drip. The chemo can destroy the mucous membranes in your nose and throat, and in the absence of nasal hair, changes the atmosphere. It's very embarrassing when you're talking to somebody and trying to not talk about cancer because you're desperate to not let it define you. Next thing you feel a drip, like somebody has turned your nose on like a tap, and you have no tissues in sight. To be honest, I got used to it in the end, until I realised it was blood dripping, (think 'L' from Stranger things) which freaked people out a bit especially the crazy three-year-old but even he got used to it, eventually. It was like my party trick (in the upside down!)

If you have ever burnt your mouth from eating hot soup, then you will have some idea of the other delightful symptom which makes your taste buds frazzle and gives you the weirdest taste in your mouth and throat. It was something I got used to, but it was pretty unbearable, most of the time. Not really properly being able to taste your food, it took me ages to fancy eating something again and craving something other than bland stodge. Even just writing about it, I can almost taste the chemo taste again. But it was just another thing to put up with, and at least my throat didn't blister all over, just down one side, so I could still eat through the pain. I don't think my taste buds or tongue have yet recovered fully, but at least I enjoy my food again now rather than eating for the sake of it. But anything spicy or crunchy, and alcohol, still trigger that burnt mouth feeling and it feels like it takes a layer off my mouth and tongue.

(Mum and Dad, if you are reading this, skip this paragraph. It's personal).

My skin was sensitive in places I never imagined. If going for a wee could sting, you can imagine wiping your bum and what that felt like. Having no pubic hair really affected the top layer of skin and it became ultra-sensitive to touch and not pleasurably. However, I'm not sure grazed labia was on the list of side effects when chemo was prescribed. Thankfully, this was short-lived!

My hands and feet became parched and itchy, and sometimes my fingers would swell. My skin was thirsty for cream and if the smell didn't make me heave, I would slather it on so thick I felt like I was sat in a bath of butter. (Thank you to those of you that bought me cream. I went through gallons of the stuff)

The chemotherapy wrecked my nails. Thankfully, I never lost them, but they came away from the nail bed halfway down the nail and were so tender. It took ages for that to grow out, but they are still very brittle and flaky, and my hands can still get so dry.

The aches and pains became unbearable. It was like having a nasty flu. It was the shooting pains that were the worst. I would wake up with pain spasms all over my body and wake Rob, who was doing a brilliant job of bringing up four kids, managing a house (full of builders and dust) and a full-time job (running a small school with students who have mental health and medical issues). He deserved a medal.

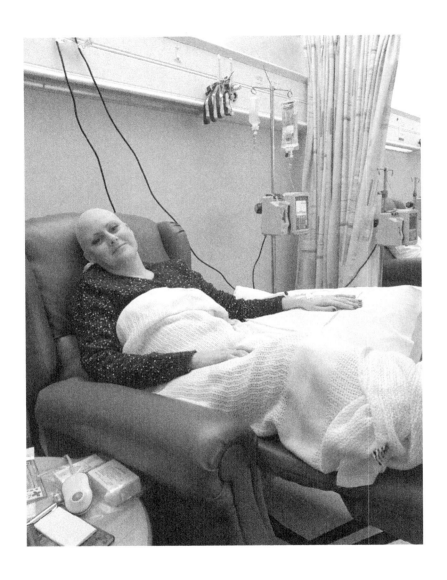

The Filgrastim was usually to blame. I knew this injection was stimulating my body to make the white blood cells that chemotherapy was killing, but I hated them and (I do not advise this) would usually only have six out of the seven prescribed because I couldn't bear them. I hope none of my medical team ever read about this! I'm sorry for wasting NHS drugs, but I just couldn't face that last one and would often hide it from Rob. Don't tell him either.

The term 'fatigue' was alien to me until this time. I'd forgotten I'd written this on my phone during the dark chemo days.

So, I'm feeling strange. Mentally. I feel jittery yet tired but can't settle. I feel really emotional and unstable and keep glimpsing a grimace on my face when I pass the mirror. My hands are shaky and I'm disorientated I'm frustrated that I can't do anything and I feel grumpy and cross. My eye is twitching like mad, my hands are freezing. As are my feet. I can't concentrate and feel things aren't achievable. I'm not in control and I don't like it. It's much easier when I can give into it, but I don't seem to. Gross taste in my mouth. I'm struggling to communicate what I want or how I feel. It's not a good day. Stabbing pains aches and chills too. I hate I can't do things. Even the loo is an effort. I'm watching people live their lives around me and I'm struggling to string a sentence together.

I spelled most of this wrong, and I only found it recently but remember it as clear as day. I can also remember thinking I'd be helpful and put a wash on. I had to throw the washing down the stairs and then shuffle kick it to the machine. Taking it out and putting it in the tumble seemed to take forever, and every movement hurt. The entire process took me all morning. I was to learn that fatigue isn't just feeling tired. It's waking up and feeling exhausted and it affects your memory, thoughts and feelings. It feels like a fog that doesn't lift all day and is so debilitating and very frustrating to live with.

The hot flushes were an utter joy! I was both freezing and cocooned in front of the fire, or half naked, looking like Mr Burns from The Simpsons. Layers on, layers off, every five minutes. I'd have the fire on for hours then be overheating and have to strip off layers of socks and blankets only to have to put them all back on again later.

These were the side effects that I experienced during my treatment and as I expressed earlier, luckily lots of patients don't suffer this badly at all. I'm amazed that some find they can still work during their regimen. I struggled to work the TV and I make no apologies for the graphic offloading of how I felt. I was fed up and miserable and just wanted it to be over, but I wasn't even halfway in!

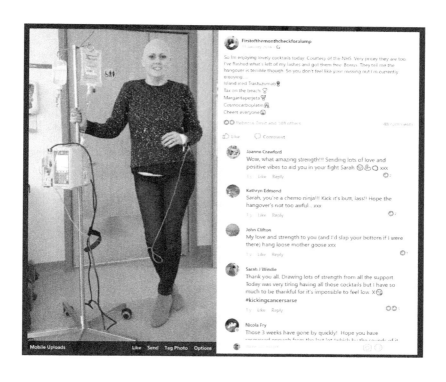

Weapons of Mass Cell Destruction

I remember little about chemo three, like the actual chemo infusions; apart from I think I'm rocking the Mrs Potato Head look in this picture. I mean, check me at going to the loo with my IV stand thing (What are they called again?) Aside from the drips, I could be holding a Porn Star Martini there, couldn't I? The strange thing is, when I see these snapshots of me living my best chemo life, I can taste the weirdness of these drugs in my throat and feel the sickness bubbling in my stomach. It's like having sensory flash backs. Spring triggers it, and certain smells. We are complex creatures, us humans.

What I remember about this Chemo is the four nights I spent in hospital with severe dehydration and being depleted in lots of nutrients (things like gin and chocolate) without giving away too much information. (Who am I kidding? You're getting all the gory details). This was the time the diarrhoea became explosive. I never thought it would hurt to poo liquid. I had days and days of explosive liquid poo juice. Nothing stayed in. Yep, this was preferable to projectile vomit, but as mentioned, we had a house full of builders and these explosions registered high on the Richter Scale. If they noticed me doing a Usain Bolt to the loo, and then rocking the foundations, they certainly kept it quiet (unlike me). I jest, but the worst I've ever felt during treatment was after this cycle.

Around this time the nosebleeds were horrendous. I looked like an extra from a horror film. In the early hours of one morning, I crawled to the bathroom whilst puking into a sick bowl. Next thing, I'm puking green bile into the bath, shitting a violent Bovril poo into the toilet, whilst projectile nose-hosing all over the floor. Again.

I remember thinking seriously... can it get any worse than this? I didn't expect to be kept in when Rob took me to A&E, but I was treated so well and was really quite poorly. In Hospital, drips were administered to rehydrate me, they gave two more injections to prevent blood clots and with the vitamin and minerals pumped back into me, my kidneys started a happy dance and I actually felt better, as you can see from these before and after pictures.

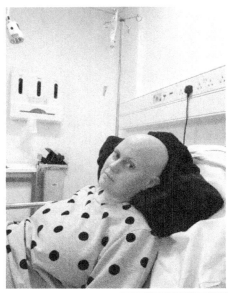

Chemo and its effect on my pathetic body really took the sail from my wings, even drinking water was a chore. It had affected my mind, and the negativity crept in. I really didn't think I could do it anymore: I had at least three more to go and my strength had gone, probably somewhere down the u-bend.

On a lighter note, there are some moments that I won't forget. When I'd arrived and before I was moved to a ward, I was in baby pink velvet PJ's with my bald head (think George Doors from Shooting Stars) and shuffling with my drip from my cubicle in A and E, to the loo about every 20 minutes. Another patient started to chat to me and seemed to be there every time I emerged to use the facilities. To say I didn't look attractive would have been an understatement, but he kept going with the compliments. "Oooh nice pyjamas" or "I saw you before didn't I, how you doing love?" then "Oh back again, I keep seeing you don't I"? He even said, "What you here for?" I think I stopped being polite pretty quickly. He was clearly self-medicating, off his face and obviously having way more fun than me. It wasn't long before I got a hit of my own as the IV anti sickness, Cyclizine, crawled through my veins and delivered some brief respite.

We had a date night on the Friday night I was in hospital. I was three days in and felt more human. We had a few snacks and watched Pretty Woman cuddled up on the hospital bed. It felt so nice to be normal. Next thing, the nurses hurried in and shut all the curtains so we couldn't see out into the corridor and other wards. We decided it was because they had brought a famous person into the hospital and they wanted privacy. I'd bet it was Ken Dodd, as he was getting on a bit. The excitement dissolved when I found out later it was because someone had died on the ward and they closed the curtains and doors because it's not great for patient morale to see one of your own has joined the afterlife. It wasn't Ken Dodd. It transpired he was to have another 18 months... sorry Ken!

This took me up to chemo four, which played out the same as the others, and as the effects are accumulative, I once again felt like the walking dead. I can remember friends coming round about ten days post chemo. I was still rough, but I found the energy to shower and changed my pyjamas in anticipation of their visit. Yet when they arrived, there was a gasp of horror when I walked into the living room and they saw me. "OMG, you look like shit", was the response. I don't think my friend, who also is a brilliant English teacher, was expecting the actual 'Boy in the Striped Pyjamas' to walk through the door, but I looked horrendous and I knew it. I was too rough to try to even do anything about it. No wig, hat or makeup would cover up how I felt, so why bother? I didn't feel the need to pretend or put on an act, which I guess is a good job as I couldn't have mustered the energy.

Unfortunately, my friend was mortified by her reaction and became tearful. I felt bad. They hadn't seen me in a while, but in all honesty; I wasn't fazed in the slightest by her comment as I did look like shit. I didn't want niceties and lies. I was glad she hadn't minced her words as I knew I looked half dead. But that's chemotherapy. Whilst cleverly killing those nasty cancer cells, it was also killing healthy cells and therefore I looked like it was slowly killing me. I enjoyed a night out the following week. What genius about oncologists is; they only give you enough poison to (nearly) kill you. Typically, you just perk up and they try to kill you again. BASTARDS!

84

It's here!! I can't quite believe how quickly these days are coming round. Chemo continues to be gruelling and I'm definitely counting down the days until it's all over. The side effects are dreadful but I have to be grateful it's working and shrinking the cancer. So I want to be honest with you all about where I'm at right now. I feel sick. Sick of feeling sick, sick of watching Rob have to do everything, sick of my pj's, sick of not being able to properly be a mum, sick of nothing tasting right, sick of my yellow baldy reflection oh and I'm really sick of daytime TV. Ok so that's enough of feeling sorry for myself (I don't, I'm just not pretending this is all a breeze) the good news is people are responding to this campaign. I'm getting messages to say people have checked and found lumps and a few have even had surgery and are awaiting test results or already have results and treatment has begun. Most people have had the all clear and just feel relieved to have been brave enough to get checked. How good is that! I'm being thanked for raising awareness. So if you're still reading this long post and have already checked today well done. If not get checking those boobs and balls. Get to know your body and then you are more likely to notice any changes. Check for visual changes too. I can't feel my cancer anymore due to massive shrinkage 🙌 but my nipple is still slightly inverted. Please comment done and share the hell out of this post so I can reach more people. I've included some pics of me when I feel rough. It's easy to share the chemo pictures of me with make up on as I feel ok then but these show the reality of chemo and I'm hoping they will encourage you to check. Thanks for reading and have a great month 👍 #firstofthemonthcheckforalump

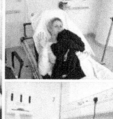

Chemo 5! Meet mrs potato head. (Thats me not my mum😆)Feeling good ATM apart from I've been told Vit D and calcium levels are very low so more drugs for that👍 If you forgot to check on the first of the month take advice from my good friend Denis Twist about checking in the middle of the month....if you get to the middle just have a fiddle😄🙂😆

👍😍🥰 Rebecca Twist and 85 others   13 comments   19 shares

👍 Like   💬 Comment   ↪ Share

6,449 people reached ›   **Boost Post**

The End is nigh!

Interestingly, chemo five was the treatment that affected me the least. I think having had so many vitamin infusions after number four, and a lovely Vitamin D booster prescription, my body seemed to recover quicker, and 7-10 days post infusion, I was feeling so much better. I'm no academic or medic, but I really think there needs to be more research done into low levels of Vitamin D and its impact on fighting disease and building immunity.

My Vitamin D levels are never good, never mind optimum. I don't know why my body dislikes it so much, but even at the end of summer, they are low. Yes, this worries me for the future. I often wonder if it contributed to me getting cancer in the first place. But I guess it is natural to want to pin it to something as otherwise you just ask yourself 'why?' all the time. All the same, it was definitely a quicker recovery time, even with the accumulative effects.

It was around this time they invited me to discuss my surgery options with a breast cancer nurse. (I was also put in touch with somebody who was on the ward and had just had the surgery I was planning to have). This meant I could get a first-hand 'warts and all' account of the procedure. I'd already met with the breast cancer consultant who had advised a full right breast mastectomy, and we had discussed removing my nipple to avoid any cheeky cells remaining. It's not uncommon to want both off when you receive a breast cancer diagnosis, as the fear of it 'spreading' to the other breast is terrifying. It was explained to me you have as much chance of getting cancer in your arm, but you wouldn't ask for that to be chopped off. It was an enlightening but fair point.

Nipple sparing was out of the equation, but I was keen and almost excited to find out my options in terms of reconstruction and what, where, when and how this could happen. It was a surprise to find out that before any major boob chopping, I would need a few lymph nodes out to check for cancer cells. This is called a 'sentinel node biopsy' and was to be a fairly quick procedure done a few weeks before my mastectomy. If no cancer cells were still dicking about in the nodes, they would remove them all during the major surgery. If not, I get to keep more of my body. It sounded like a good trade off to me.

I'm not sure anyone realises how much logistical planning goes into these surgeries and how many options and variables there are.

It's a complex business and we are so privileged to have a variety of options, but when faced with these confusing choices, the decisions have huge implications on your physical and mental health.

- They offered me:
- No reconstruction
- An implant (but this I would have to wait for, as you can't have one before radiotherapy)
- Diep flap reconstruction (to use my belly fat to make a new boob)

- Other fat transfer reconstruction, but these weren't an option as I didn't have enough back or thigh fat, apparently. (I think this was debatable).

All the procedures were explained in full by the plastics breast cancer nurse, who was warm, supportive and lovely, whilst also realistic about what this could entail.

It was a straightforward decision for me, to be honest. I 'loved' the sound of the Diep flap reconstruction. A boob job and tummy tuck in one go? What could go wrong? Why wouldn't everyone opt for this? Well, because it is a very personal choice, for a start. And I now respect that everyone has different priorities and preferences. The surgery I was choosing came with risk. It was a very long and complicated procedure involving two surgical teams. With the fat, they have to take a network of blood vessels and attach them to vessels in your chest. Think 'Build a Bear' but without the 'Sparkly Wishing Star'. This doesn't always work, and the cells can die, meaning possibly more surgery to remove them. I had to be scanned to map out these blood vessels and check my C-section scar was not in the way. Obviously, the skill required should not be compared to stuffing a bear, although I think the cost of the surgery isn't too far removed from a trip to 'Build a Bear'!

I'm not sure that I knew what I was letting myself in for, but was desperate for something good to come out of this entire business, and why not? I hadn't asked to get cancer, why not be disillusioned and assume I would end up with the perfect body too! So, the Diep option was my decision, and this is what we planned for. It was also confirmed from seeing my new friend, who was three days post procedure and recovering well. I'd only met her for five minutes before she shared her war wounds. I guess we were in the 'Cancer Club' and you become complacent about who sees what after not very long. The wound was neat, and she was feeling well, so that was enough for me.

They pencilled my surgery in. I just had to endure another (but my last) chemo first and God, was that tough.

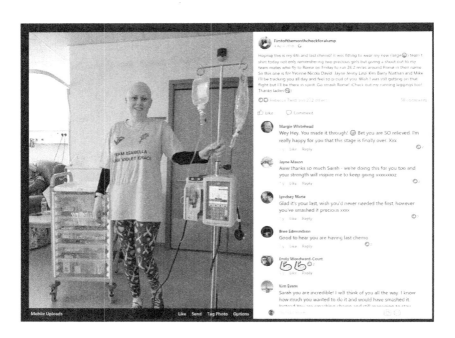

Your home should provide respite from the hustle and bustle of the outside world

Relax in a favourite chair or curl up in a generous sofa with a good book.

Create a haven

Take time out

individual style.

in the bedroom

Last of my Chemo Marathons

I was desperate to finish by the time they infused my last chemical cocktail. By now I hated it. The smell of the 'Sanicloth' wipes, the pre-chemo steroid insomnia, the painted smile that made my cheeks ache, to wondering will they get the IV in my weak, pathetic veins first attempt this time. I felt sick by association.

My running club mates were about to go to Rome to run our second international marathon, yet my marathon was nearing its end and I was more than exhausted. I still had FOMO. I wanted to be well enough to have done the training and feel part of the team. To board that plane in anticipation and go to the expo and pasta party, was what I really wanted to be doing. But it wasn't to be. As I have said before, I had to suck it up. I was at my worst that Sunday morning and although I was following them on the tracking app; I was struggling to lift my head off the pillow from the usual combination of hellish side effects. It was one of those times I was literally counting down the minutes.

Out of the blue, I received a video call from three of the group who were running together and messaging me. I sobbed as I saw their lovely, sweaty faces and was thrilled they had shared a bit of their day and run with me. The atmosphere was clearly electric. However, it looked tough and boiling, but in equal measure, I think we spurred each other on that day, and it was a real comfort that they made contact. In fact, I will never forget it.

A few days later, the builders decided this was the time to break a hole through the landing ceiling to fit the stairs for our loft conversion, and I was still feeling ropey. This was the point in the renovation that dust couldn't be contained to one place and sealed off. So, the decision was made to pack me and my daughter off to a dust/builder-free hotel for a bit of respite. It cost a small fortune, but it was bliss. I couldn't enjoy the time with her like I really wanted to, but the hotel staff were really kind and upgraded us. They couldn't have been more accommodating. I remember feeling really sad though that aged eleven she was having to look after me, tucking me in bed and turning out the light. I hadn't told her (or Rob when he called) that my temperature had gone up and that I should ring the hospital. I'd decided (with all my medical expertise) to see if I could sleep it off and thank goodness I did.

When I returned to the house, it wasn't as dusty and I was slowly feeling better, although it seemed to take ages, after this last chemo, to bounce back.

I had a few appointments over the next few weeks, but the best part of ending chemo, at that point, was I could travel to London for the day to support Rhona, running the London marathon. She had been amazing throughout, and I really wanted to surprise her by rocking up with the support team from the running group. I don't know about everyone that ran 26.2 miles in the blistering heat that day, but when I look back, I'm not sure how I did it as a spectator. I slept a lot that following week, but I loved every minute; and being normal again, for a while.

She admits to being cross with me for turning up unexpectedly and pretending I was back home in bed. That was the hottest London Marathon on record, and they actually ran out of water. Well, these girls can; and she certainly finished and did herself proud that day, and I don't regret that I was there to see it. Look how much fun we all had and check out my shiny head. I look like I've been photo shopped into that picture.

I had ten days after that to rest before my sentinel node biopsy surgery on the 3rd May and had a confirmed date for 21st May for the Diep reconstruction and Mastectomy. Not long to wait to look like a cancer free Goddess. Things were looking up, and I felt like I was climbing slowly out of a deep crater... Bring it on!

Firstofthemonthcheckforalump
1 May 2018 ·

I've spent ages this morning looking for poignant messages/images about Breast cancer. There's a lot of pink fluff and smut. (I've attached examples as proof!) not a great deal of information out there that isn't repeated but if I've learnt anything these past few months it's that BC comes in many different forms and certainly isn't just a lump even though I'm aware that's what I ask you to check for. (I still love the lemons)The most important message is to get to know your body by looking and feeling and noticing any changes. Colour, shape, texture. A lot of you will have changes during your cycle so work out when the best time of the month is for you to check. Also extend your check to armpits if don't don't already. Don't be shy going to your GP as most lumps/changes don't end up being cancer but it's better to get in early in case it is as it's much easier to treat. I'm now chemo free and pray I never need it again although I'm told it can take months for side effects to bugger off. I had my first herceptin injection a week ago and will have this every three weeks for a year. It is a targeted therapy for HER2 BC And stops the cells duplicating so it is my (stingy) friend Thursday brings my first surgery. They will remove some lymph nodes to see if I still have cancer in them and decide how many to take during my mastectomy. I'm hoping the chemo has blasted them but if not I will gift them to the NHS along with my boob! So please check and share. If anyone had already remembered that it was the first and checked without this reminder can you let me know. Also please please share. We could be saving a life! Thanks again to everyone who has read this and continuous to support me. I'm getting there

The surgery before THE surgery

"We injected some blue dye into your breast to help us identify the lymph nodes in your arm pit. This blue dye will give you a pale grey appearance in the first 24 hours after the operation. You may also notice your urine is a bright green colour, for the first day or two, as the dye leaves your body."

I wasn't shocked to wake up from my sentinel node biopsy with a blue boob, as I had been warned that this Smurf transition would happen. I had a slight 'corpse-green' tinge to my complexion for a day or so, and I was totally expecting to look like Mama Smurf. Luckily, the surgery was straightforward, and I was back to normal pretty quickly. The green wee was just another thing to laugh at. I had learnt pretty quickly you have to laugh at yourself and the situation as the alternative was to be a maudlin cancer victim and I wasn't taking that role in my script. Thankfully, I had a very neat scar in my armpit where they had removed three lymph nodes. It was sore, but nothing a few paracetamol couldn't sort out.

The results of the biopsy on the lymph nodes, to check if I needed a full node clearance during my mastectomy, came back quickly and to discover that that there was no cancer present in any of the three nodes they whipped out was brilliant news. Hurrah! I was beating this cancer back into its dirty little corner.

As hoped, a little more of my body would stay intact and I now had 10 days to wait until my mastectomy and Diep flap reconstruction.

Although I was still very fatigued from the six-months of treatment, I was determined to have a few days of relative normality before I was to be turned into the bride of Frankenstein. When I say normality, most days were taken up with appointments in various hospitals.

First was the pre-op, where you sit and wait to be called in by various medical staff for blood tests, urine sample, ECG, etc. On this occasion, two staff came out at the same time and asked for Sarah Vaughan. I felt they were actually fighting over me until one of them took me through to the consulting room. I then wondered why the surgery details were being repeated and then discussion started about a completely different procedure that I had certainly not signed up for. When they checked my date of birth, they soon realised they had the wrong person. They wanted a Sarah Bourne for this surgery, whom presumably was sitting patiently in the waiting room. What are the odds of two clinicians coming into the waiting room requesting Sarah Vaughan and Sarah Bourne simultaneously? Thank God it wasn't calling us into theatre, and they were removing her arm, I'd have been really lopsided. (DISCLAIMER... OUR WONDERFUL NHS WOULD OBVS NEVER DO THIS. I'VE EMBELISHED THIS THEATRE BIT TO MAKE MY STORY FUNNIER) Although, the amount of triple checking of name and date of birth, it's obvious this has happened in the past!

Other appointments involved a wound surgery follow up, and all was fine. I had to have my results appointment with the breast cancer surgeon and check everything was in place for the 21st.

I also had my first injection of Herceptin the 'targeted therapy' that would ensure that the type of cancer I had (HER2 positive) would not return. I won't lie, the various appointments had become something of a comfort to me. All the to-ing and fro-ing to different hospitals was reassuring, as I knew these people had my back. Be it an echocardiogram or pre-chemo review appointments with the oncologist, I'd felt looked after and safe.

They had warned me that this Herceptin injection was likely to sting, but what I hadn't realised was that the injection was in my leg for up to 4 minutes while the drugs slowly dispersed into my bloodstream. Apparently the longer it takes, the less it hurts. I can confirm, after a year of these, that I'd totally agree. And the quicker the needle is pushed in, the more the stingy little bugger hurts. I had to be grateful I was offered this 'thousand-pound-a-time' treatment. Until recently it was a postcode lottery who received it. I can't imagine how that must feel, knowing that at the area you live in could dictate ultimately, whether you live or die.... how bloody horrific.

I was grateful and privileged to have access to all this treatment, the consultations, the surgeries, the warmth, sympathy and care. I was lucky to have this and that it was on my doorstep. Literally ten minutes to both hospitals and I still don't take this for granted. Although in the weeks following my surgery, I think I took it for granted, I felt very sorry for my hunched over, swelled-up, knackered body and I was very 'Zimmer frame' grumpy.

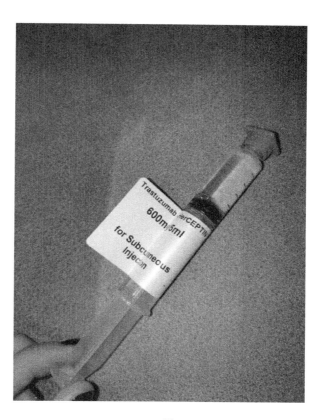

Mastectomy Surgery

So, I drank too much Prosecco on the Saturday before my surgery. There, I said it. I feel better now, but please don't try this at home. Or judge me. We always went for a break with friends on this May weekend, to a Haven caravan. The kids loved it; we loved it; it was cheap and safe (if that can come in the same sentence) and it felt like a wonderful time to have a bit of fun. I felt giddy by the lovely weather and the Royal Wedding, but I woke up on the Sunday morning, my 44th Birthday, feeling very guilty, scared and nervous for the dice and slice that was to come the following day. We didn't stick around and packed up with a headache and sick feeling from nervous anxiety that was infiltrating my body (or boozy Saturday.) I knew I was due in hospital that night for my pre surgery checks and powdered drinks (to keep me hydrated through the surgery!) I realise how bad that sounds now, but I drank a lot of water that day to compensate.

We tried to make the best of the day, but early evening I got the call that the room and hospital were ready for me and so off I went. I decorated my hospital room with my birthday cards and ate some chocolate whilst waiting for my surgeon to come and draw on me with his sandwich bag of markers. I kid you not, my husband bought him some sharpies and a pencil case after this as a treat! I posted a picture of vandalised me onto Facebook that night and it is to date my most shared post and has reached people all over the world! It's so hard to raise awareness, and it's not the messages you think would inspire people to check that always do.

I had been washing with a medical shower gel for the past few days to ward off or kill super bugs like MRSA, so I couldn't even enjoy a nice hot bath in preparation as I needed my medical scrub, which didn't exactly smell of roses.

This picture is gross. I'd put on so much weight from the steroids and encouraged to grow this belly for my new boob. I'll admit now, I slept little that night because of the waves of terror rolling over me. Plus, when you are not ill, those beds are more motel than hotel, just so very uncomfortable and noisy. However, everyone was so nice to me and managed a laugh whilst being supportive and sympathetic as I was spending my birthday evening incarcerated in 'Hotel Whiston'..

I'll be honest, all my bravado was gone by the time I walked to the operating theatre the following morning and said goodbye to Rob. I sobbed. Both surgeons hugged me, but the amount of people coming in to introduce themselves was overwhelming. I'm not usually bothered by surgery or an anaesthetic, but this felt like the big deal it was and fear took over. How amazing are these people though? Everyone had a role, busying themselves around me in a friendly, comfortable way. Next thing I remember was waking up in recovery, shivering and with supports on my legs, that inflated to keep my circulation going, (I'd had a lazy few hours) like hot inflatable cricket pads only one wasn't working and I remember saying "It's not working, it's not working".

I know from previous experience that I waffle when coming round in recovery, but I'm not sure what happened this time as I was very drowsy from being under for twelve hours. There was a really caring nurse, efficiently making me comfortable, whilst faffing round, removing wires and adjusting breathing tubes. He was so nice, reassuring and professional, and I felt safe. I guess it's hard to thank these people as they see you drugged up, talking shite, and then you go off to the ward and they apply the same amount of professionalism and care to the next person. I remember a nurse saying, "Oh! I've just seen you on Facebook. Are you doing that campaign?" Which was amazing, but weird? I remember hearing the surgeon speaking to Rob on the phone as he was obviously worried. Rob, not the surgeon!

I don't know how I managed a Facebook post that night, but I did,

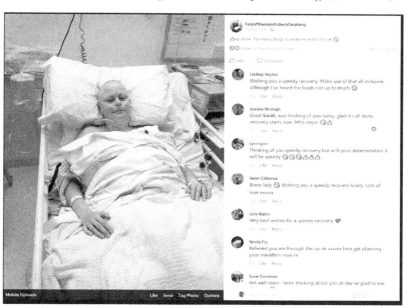

once back on the ward. Rob couldn't stay long as he'd been waiting ages for me, but I wasn't in a fit state for company as I was still quite drugged up. I was being checked and scanned with a doppler every five minutes to see if the tissue was still alive, so I don't think I had any quality sleep at all that night. I woke up to Rob returning before he went to work, and he encouraged me to eat a bit of breakfast. My lovely friend Rhona appeared before her shift and said "Jesus, you look like shit". I really like this kind of honesty because yes, I was grey, and I did!

During the early check that morning, the surgeon thought I may need a blood transfusion as I obviously had a corpse-like aura. He also told me to not eat and drink in case I needed further surgery that day, as my new toob (tummy boob) was looking a bit swollen. I was pleased about the transfusion news as it was an amazing feeling after my c-section, when they gave me four units, so I was fully expecting this feeling of being reborn again. I wasn't thrilled that I could need further surgery, however. Wasn't 12 hours enough? The blood tests that came back (when three people later they could get a line in me) showed that yes, I needed two units. Unfortunately, they were given during the surgery to remove the ever-growing blood mass in my new boob. Think Augustus Gloop, and you can imagine what my boob was now looking like. Another four hours of surgery was ticked off, and by now I felt really poorly. I had a lot of anaesthesia, but my Diep incision and general stomach area were so sore. I was told the small tube that was woven into the incision providing local anaesthetic should be dealing with that pain, but it really wasn't, and the liquid morphine (Oramorph) was just about keeping it manageable.

The blur of the Tuesday night monitoring and probing, turning into Wednesday morning monitoring and probing, brought little relief. I wasn't eating but becoming more and more bloated. I have never felt so out of control in my life. I couldn't move, I couldn't feel much other than pain. I was attached to four drains and had been catheterised. I felt sick, bloated and bunged up. I was tired, emotional, hot and exhausted. I couldn't reach my buzzer for more pain relief, so felt trapped and claustrophobic. I would slip down in the bed and didn't have any control of my 'shark bite core' to move myself up. I was slowly being cooked on the 'baking tray' hospital bed. The staff were obviously rushed off their feet, but it was hours at one point before anyone came to see me, and I think by then I was sobbing.

Things got a little worse through the night, and the next morning I was throwing up everywhere. I can't tell you how much I still hated being sick. Vomiting after all that surgery was just impossible. I didn't have the muscle support and constantly felt like I was choking on my vomit. It seemed like ages, but I eventually got some IV anti sickness and fluids and from this point the worst had passed. I built my strength up and began eating and drinking again.

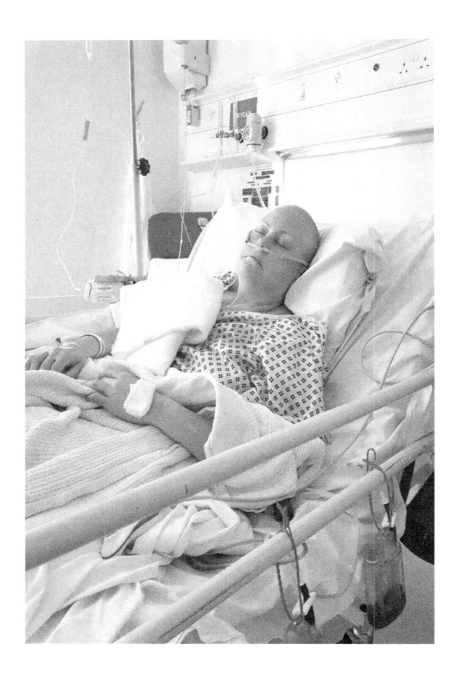

By the Thursday morning, they realised the reason for my Diep pain was because the pump attached to the line in me, supposedly delivering local anaesthetic, had never worked. It was one of those things and no one's fault but it explained why I had been in so much pain. Therefore, I was demanding the Oramorph hit, which I hadn't realised was making me bunged up, sick and low.

To add insult to injury, I woke up at one point to find the canula in my hand, delivering the fluids, had popped out of the vein and my hand was filling up with saline and the tape was popping off. I was screaming for someone to come and help me, but my buzzer was on the floor (again) and no one could hear me. I had a massive hand by the time someone came in, but thankfully they were not worried. When the canula came out, so did the fluid-spurting out in a big arch from the back of my hand, like someone had pierced a water balloon! You can also see the effects of the chemo on my nails in this picture.

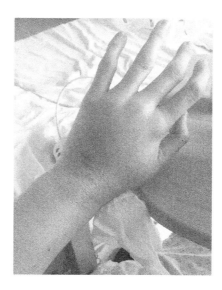

You couldn't write it! Apart from that fact that I just did. I have to say that the nurses in the plastics ward were truly amazing souls. They are so understaffed but were wonderful with me, and it was that human touch that got me through one of the worst weeks of my life. When I write about these mishaps, I don't blame anyone; it was just the way it went that week.

I impressed everyone with my new boob, but I was more concerned with the four drains, catheter and shark bite incision across my stomach. It felt so tight, I didn't think I'd ever be able to stand up again. The physiotherapists were polite but firm, it felt so very hard to take any steps and they are quite persistent. I couldn't remember a word they said to me about the exercises I had to do and I'm ashamed to say, I would put it off because it hurt too much. But it came to a point where I just wanted to get out of there, so I dug deep and took the steps challenge. I was like Jet from Gladiator but with surgical stockings and a Zimmer frame (I nearly had pressure sores on my heels from being flat for so long in the hot hospital room.) Thank you to the weather Gods for the twenty-five degrees that week.

As the days wore on, I got that bit stronger and managed a shower and had my drains out. So, after six nights, all-inclusive in Hotel Whiston, two surgeries, many units of blood, fluid and a litre of Oramorph, I was off to the homestead to see my family and 'sleep' in my own bed. It was the most expensive hotel I've ever stayed in and whilst all the staff were wonderful, I wouldn't rate the food or bed for comfort, or a relaxing break.

Shark bites and eyelashes! 👀

If anyone finds my dummy bin it ive thrown it far😩 I'm not in a good mood today because I'm still sore from the surgery and can't fit into my clothes because of swelling. (Not to mention the compression socks I still have to wear) and my independence is low☹ See I'm a grumpy bugger. I know it's done and I'm probably cancer free and I should be singing from the roof tops but I'm not because I want to be able to go out and be normal. I think I left my patience on the operating table😵 I know I'm sooo much better off than lots of people and have a lot to look forward to but for now I'm grumpy and tired and sore and frustrated. BUT it's the first of the Month so I've decided to hold you all to ransom with my mood by checking for those lumps or changes to your breasts and testicles (if you have both then it's double the work fellas) by now you should be getting to know your body and be more familiar with any changes. Remember it's not just lumps my cancer was a hard mass, other people report dimpling or a rash or discharge. Be body aware, check and share. You never know I may have cheered up and stopped feeling sorry for myself by the time you've checked😄 in other news ....I have new eyelashes. Off to suck it up and get on with it. Firstofthemonthcheckforalump

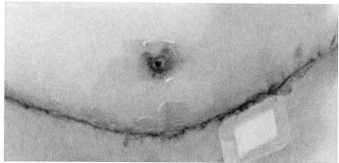

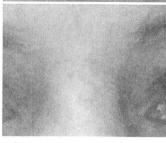

BREAST SELF EXAMINATION

 Write a comment   📷 ☺

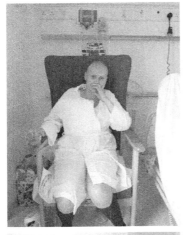
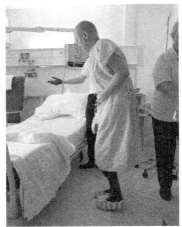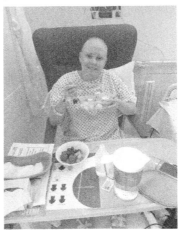

Surgery Recovery

Whilst my account of surgery is dramatic and traumatic, and I feel it's important not to sugar-coat it, I certainly don't regret my decision. I have spoken to many people since who haven't had a negative experience and have recovered really quickly, especially those who have this before treatment.

I'm sharing this not to put anyone off. I hadn't really prepared myself for how debilitating I would feel, and I was also just unlucky in how it unfolded that week. Even at home, it seemed at the time to take an age to heal and I was fed up, as you can sense in my June 1st Facebook post. I was so impatient for some normality and really resented things, like having to wear surgical socks for six weeks to prevent blood clots. Especially as the summer was hot, sticky and long. I got minor infections in both wounds, probably from trying to do too much too soon, and I was very sore and irritable. I don't think after the poison of chemo my body wanted to catch up to my mind, and why should it? Maybe there was a lesson to be learned in there somewhere.

I remember about 10 days after surgery I was chatting to my daughter in her room and I just sobbed for what felt like an eternity. If I'm honest, this was the first time I'd had a really good cry and felt sorry for myself since my diagnosis and it felt good to release all the emotion. I was so sore and miserable; I couldn't find a comfortable position to sleep in and it felt never ending. I kept doubting my decision to have this procedure and feeling like I had been vain, but I'd never even considered not having a reconstruction. My usual positive outlook and persona was shrinking with the stitches that had become tight and itchy, and the reaction to the huge sticky dressings meant my skin was on fire. But there was good news ahead. The surgeon was impressed with how everything had settled, and I got the histology report back to confirm that there was no evidence of cancer in any of the breast tissue they removed. The chemo cocktail and my body had won over cancer. I was nearly there with my treatment and bloody cancer free. YES! It was me against the world now, and I was moving forward.

F**K YOU, CANCER

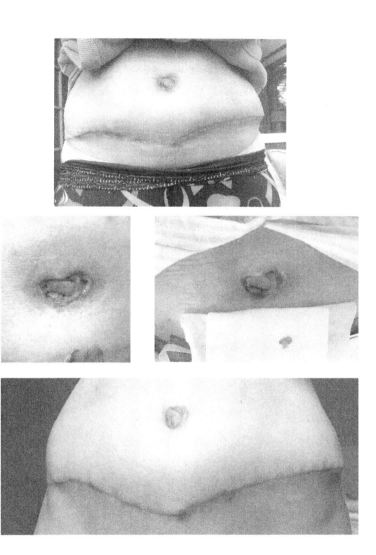

Firstofthemonthcheckforalump
6 July 2018 · G

The aliens got me again! 3 down 12 to go👍

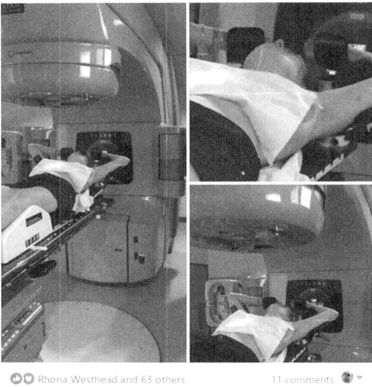

 Like   💬 Comment   ➦ Share

1,071 people reached ›

Boost Post

Apathy killed the Radiotherapy Star

I had six weeks in between surgery and the start of radiotherapy, and by this point in my treatment, the anger at my situation had kicked in. It was a total pity party of "Why me"? Life isn't fair. Everyone said it was a breeze compared to chemo, and it was. It didn't hurt, didn't make me sick. So, what was my problem?

My first trip to Clatterbridge was to get me all set up for radiotherapy and I found the experience very scary and unsettling. I'd been lucky that my chemo was at our local hospital, which was a satellite centre for Clatterbridge, so I hadn't had to travel there every day or week, like some people. It was an old building and a bit of a minefield to navigate, with strange corridors linking old and new sites, and there was something really tragic about the frail, bald and really sick people sitting waiting to hear their fate.

It was the first time I'd seen the cancer bell and heard someone ring it, to mark the end of chemo, and it gave me goose bumps. Then there was the therapy dog, which I found disconcerting, as I wasn't a dog person and didn't know they existed. I actually recognised three people whilst I was there. Two of whom have since passed away. It had taken me seven months, but the reality of my situation hit me. I was at this point really grateful for the modern, warm and friendly Lilac Centre and its staff. It wasn't clinical or intimidating there, unlike how Clatterbridge felt. I felt like a cancer patient and I felt I looked like one.

After everything I'd been through so far, I thought I'd cope ok with what was to happen next. I was to have a scan and be measured up for my radiotherapy so that when I was microwaved; the radiation hit the right spot.

It's hard to explain how the next half an hour went. It was intrusive, claustrophobic and frightening. I hadn't done my research. I hadn't realised they would make a mask by forming thermoplastic around my chin to strap me in and down. I didn't realise I'd have to have my hands behind my head for an eternity (a 20-minute eternity). I didn't realise I'd have to breathe in and hold it for a certain amount of time so that lasers could measure the exact spot. I didn't realise the pin prick tattoos I was given to line me up would hurt, and I had four of them. I didn't realise I'd be lying there in my knickers. I didn't realise I'd feel like I was in the film 'Alien' being experimented on. However, I guess I looked like Sigourney Weaver. The entire experience was uncomfortable and surprising, and I felt violated.

Fast forward a few weeks, and I was on my way to Aintree, this time for my treatment. I was feeling thankful for another satellite clinic. This facility was, like the Lilac Centre, brand spanking new and all top spec. It was a pleasant place with bright airy waiting rooms and a lovely garden to sit in, if the weather played in your favour. It had a Macmillan area with lots of reading material or support, if you needed it, and a café, which was just as well as the machines, all 2.5-million-pound worth, break down a lot. Often, I'd wait up to 2 hours to get into Birch or Blossom (they named the rooms). When you go into the changing room you are supposed to change into your gown, but I was never given one for the three weeks I was there so the first time I arrived in a summer dress I had to sit in my knickers waiting to lie on the table. All my details were on a screen that gave the radiographers the measurements for my treatment. They moved me and gently shoved and nudged me to match up my tattoo dots and a pen mark, just below my neck, that they taped over. With the hot weather, it rarely lasted a day, so I'd have to be pre-measured for that every day, which unfortunately, took extra time. There was a lot of adjusting as they continued to move me, clipping me in by my thermoplastic mask and then manoeuvring the table under the machine. A screen, similar to a TV on a plane, was pulled down so I could see three electronic lines, and when breathing in and holding my breath, the coloured block needed to hover over the middle line so they could administer the radiotherapy. It was all very surreal and although it didn't hurt, I really didn't enjoy feeling so exposed.

After a few days, I had a word with myself. I was cancer free at this point and this was an insurance policy. There were people there whose only chance was this treatment and needed over fifteen zaps (three weeks). I often drove myself there and back but would come home and sleep. It was really tiring being microwaved every day, and the sunburnt feeling I was left with needed a serious amount of cream to stop it blistering. Otherwise, that was it!

We had to go to a talk about Lymphedema, which can cause swelling in your affected arm after surgery and radiotherapy, and they taught us exercises that would help and gave information on what to watch out for. I was the naughty one at the back who was told off for not doing my exercises properly, or frequently enough. I didn't much fancy a massive arm though, so I tried. I honestly did. Because I've had lymph nodes removed this is something I need to watch out for going forward. I'm not advised to have injections or blood tests taken in my right arm and must make sure any cuts are kept clean and dressed.

Even though radiotherapy was nothing to get stressed out about, I still hated it, and when I rang that bell on my last treatment, I sobbed. I was so relieved it was all over (apart from my Herceptin). I could now get back to some sort of normality and live my life again.

Firstofthemonthcheckforalump
24 July 2018 · 🌐

Yes!!!

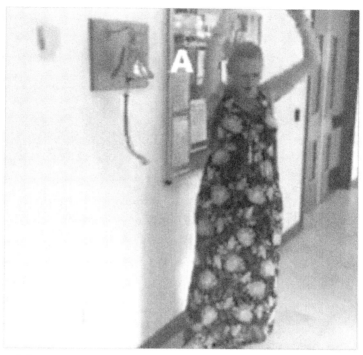

We're all going on a Summer Holiday

I was so pleased that after everything we could still go on our family holiday that was booked way before my diagnosis. I felt it was important for us all, as a family, to spend this time together; to be normal – to have fun. And we did. It was a bit crap not being able to expose my right side to the sun, or go in the pool, but a small price to pay for being together, away in the sun.

I didn't care that it exposed my shark bite. People could think what they liked. I felt so lucky to be alive. Yes, I was shattered after everything my body and mind had been through, but I would not let that spoil this precious time away. This was the point I decided I was going to write this book about my experiences and campaign to raise awareness. I was doing it for myself, but I wondered if I could ever reach and help anyone else by being brutally honest. I was going to be positive and try, as I couldn't lose anything.

On our return, I was booked in for a bone scan and I was also still having my three weekly Herceptin injections, and these weren't without their side effects. Mainly for me, I woke up in the morning like the Tin Man. I'm sure, on reflection, I should have carried a can of oil round with me. Other side effects like headaches and diarrhoea, where just part and parcel of the leftovers of chemo and weren't bad enough to be debilitating. It was the joint pain and fatigue that was my nemesis. I couldn't get through the day without a 'nana nap'.

People see you with your pixie crop and know you've finished treatment and ticked the surgery box, so assume you're good to go. It doesn't quite work like that for everyone. My body was trying to adjust to a new normal and my mind was trying to play catch up with everything I'd been through over the last ten months. Outwardly, I was smiling and looking less like a poisoned Russian, but inside, I was trying to find myself again. Trying to function as the new me wasn't easy, but I was trying really hard to grasp everything, as best I could, and move forward. My brain just didn't work as it did and my memory was, and still is, awful.

I was feeling under pressure from HR to return to work, but I knew I wasn't ready and was advised by my breast cancer nurse that it was going to take time to come to terms with what I'd been through, both the physical and emotional recovery. I was craving some normality, but I didn't really know what that meant anymore. Did I want to return to teaching? What was my path now? Was cancer sent so I could save the world?

Luckily, I had the support of a counsellor to talk through a lot of unanswered questions. Why me? What if it's not gone? What if it comes back? Although my strong positive approach to dealing with the big C had got me through until now, it was only seeing this counsellor that made me admit I had suffered trauma. In fact, the trauma had begun a lot earlier than my diagnosis and it was only now reflecting on some past events that I realised a few things about myself. I wasn't cancer Sarah; I wasn't pre-cancer Sarah, so what bloody Sarah was I?

I knew and could reflect on the attitude I'd had and the fact I had turned a negative into a positive, by raising awareness through my #FIRSTOFTHEMONTHCHECKFORALUMP campaign, was something I was really proud of. It was around this time I realised I wanted to do something much more than a small blog on Facebook. If I'd realised how hard it was to get people to listen (or hear) the message, I'm not sure at that point I'd have had the energy to develop anything.

I realised how much family members, particularly my daughter, had been affected by my diagnosis, and in my hurry to be positive and get on with it, I'd maybe ignored the fact that this wasn't or hadn't been as easy for them as I'd thought. My daughter had just started secondary school and was really struggling with what appeared to be school based anxiety. The transition from primary to secondary is never easy as suddenly a school world that is very comfortable, where children are big fish in a small pond, was gone. They face being tiny sticklebacks in a swirling murky (and smelly) lake. We have all had to do it and a certain amount of fear is normal, but I think if there has been any trauma around this transition time and that isn't supported, we can set our young people up for a bumpy road.

So, for my daughter, who had gone from being an only child for eight years, to now having an adoptive brother, not living with her dad, gaining two stepbrothers, a stepdad and moving into a new house, to find out her mum has breast cancer, starting secondary school was the straw that broke the camel's back.

Luckily, it was a storm we all rode together (not on the camel) and she came through that time stronger, with a better understanding of herself.

But it made me think. If I had died (God forbid) there would have been no end of support for my family. There are now so many more of us survivors because treatment has improved, and we are thankfully living for longer. But what support is out there for our children or our parents or partners? There is very little, and so my idea of setting up a charity to support survivor's families was indeed born. At the time I had no idea when or how I was going to do that, as I already felt like time was running out for all the ideas I had and wanted to act upon. I also felt panicky in my quest to achieve them. The clock felt like it was certainly ticking.

Firstofthemonthcheckforalump
3 January · 🌐 ···

How brilliant is this. I received this message and was sad to hear of another diagnosis but thrilled that by raising awareness it was found in the first place. I always said if I could help just one person i would be thrilled but I've had many like this over the past year. How amazing. Read on and thank you to the lady who shared this with me. 😊

"You are an inspiration. It was thru Reading yr story in The Liverpool Echo that prompted me to start checking. Bec of yr prompting and my persistence my BC was discovered at stage 3. Thank you so much for highlighting your own journey which brought me to discover mine. Idve posted this much sooner but I've only just posted abt my journey on my page for the first time since my diagnosis. Please don't ever underestimate the fantastic work you do in spreading yr story and raising awareness. Bec I am prob just one of many who acted upon it and you have probably saved my life, saved my three children from being motherless and my husband from being a widower. That's the reality. So a huge thank you 😊 💙💙💙 💙"

👍❤️👏 Rhona Westhead and 111 others   16 comments 6 shares 🐶 ▾

👍 Like   💬 Comment   ↪ Share

2,110 people reached ›

Boost Post

125

Spreading the Word to the Facebook World

It had become apparent that although I didn't really have the foggiest how to blog, my message was getting out. I was getting some great feedback online and in person, which inspired me to continue. Don't get me wrong, I often thought I should stop ramming breast cancer down people's throat and I considered if it was good for my mental health to keep "going on about it". Maybe it was time to "move on and get on with my life".

Then I thought, bollocks to that! This campaign wasn't stopping me from getting on with my life or moving on and forward and it was actually helping me. It wasn't maudlin, and I wasn't wallowing. I realised that helping people made me feel good. No, actually it made me feel amazing, especially when I received messages from people thanking me. Just read some of these now and imagine how you would feel. It saddened me that other people were potentially going through what I went through, but they were thanking me for raising awareness and potentially saving their lives. How bloody amazing is that? These are some messages I've received.

"You should be proud of how you handled yourself then and continuously since. I'd forgotten how poorly you looked to be honest. Your positive outlook and strength have helped so many ladies. I went to the docs on the back of your prompts last year and my lump was a cyst thankfully. Keep doing what you do and stay well."

"I didn't want to comment on your page because although my diagnosis isn't a secret, I'm not ready for Facebook to know. Because of following your page, I've checked my boobs regularly. At the end of March, I found a lump. I've now had a lumpectomy and lymph removal. I got my results yesterday, and they were positive in that the cancer hasn't spread. I've got to have chemo and radio, though. But that's ok. I can do that. The reason for my message is firstly to thank you and secondly to ask if you know of local support groups in the area?"

"Hi Sarah, we've never met, but I knew your story and follow your firstofthemonth campaign. I just want to say a big thankyou for doing it as it really does put it in my mind and whereas I prob checked annually before, I do check more regularly now. Which is great because I did find a little twatty lump earlier this month and I'm now in the system with surgery in a couple of weeks. You're doing a great service love, wishing you a healthy happy 2020 love from **** x"

"Hey, I don't know you but a mutual friend added me to the group months ago and I've watched your progress with admiration for you (having lost a dear friend a few years back) I saw your post today and when I was showering tonight, I remembered it and checked myself, and I've found a lump (large marble size) which I'm now going to get checked out properly tomorrow. There's a history of non nasty lumps with both

127

my mother and her sister when they were around my age so I'm trying not to worry too much, but I wanted to thank you for your post as I almost definitely wouldn't have checked myself without seeing it. I'm keeping my fingers crossed.xxx

Wow! You are an inspiration and a saviour to so many. If not for you i would not have been aware of the less reported signs of breast cancer "nipple bleeding". Thankfully and praise be I'm post surgery and all clear. My heartfelt thanks to you and only you. Dream big gorgeous girl. X Forgot to say..I triggered concern on the 3rd of the month post your post and called the doc that same day. Xxx The rest is as above,,, Thank you a million times.

My friend told me about u hun. Ur story helped me to stay strong and focused thank u xx U r doin an amazing thing. We need more people like u. Cus I found it so early it was 17mm when they took it out I only need radio and the hormone tablet xx

We don't know each other but you are amazing for all that you are doing on ur page while fighting that's shitty cancer. I keep watching seeing where ur up to. I think ur so amazing and beautiful and if I had half ur strength I'd be made up and I'm not fighting any fight. You are an inspiration to all around I will keep following you and fight with you and send all I have 💚 you don't need to me say but you are doing bloody amazing 🤍 💚 🤍 💚 🤍 💚 🖤

Your journey is very inspirational. I'm a poor checker because my doctor scared the life out of me once and I'm afraid to check now. I will check regular I promise! Good luck tomorrow I'm sure you'll be great. I hope it goes well. Keep smiling, you're amazing! Thank you for making me aware.

What changes do you look for?

TEXTURE

WEEPING

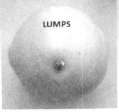

LUMPS

CHANGES TO SHAPE

REDNESS

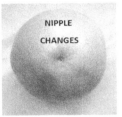

NIPPLE CHANGES

OR JUST SWELLING

BE BREAST AWARE

Get into the habit of checking at the same time every month (note natural changes in your cycle) and include the armpits as well as boobs. Cancer caught early is easier to treat and most lumps turn out to be benign. If in doubt check it out with your GP.

 facebook **#firstofthemonthcheckforalump**

Designs for Life

It was a natural progression to design a poster to spread the word. My idea of having the posters on the back of toilet doors was short-lived, as it seems people just don't want to know. It didn't stop me though. Even though I knew they would eventually be taken down, if they had reached a few people, having a read whist they were having a wee, then job done. I didn't want them to be pink as this had been done before, but I wanted them to be informative and highlight what to look for.

So, it began. I bought a couple of bags of oranges and began photographing them with different backgrounds. I manipulated the shapes to show lumps and bumps and mixed syrup for the nipple bleeding. I moved some boxes to make space (we hadn't pimped up this room yet), set up a little studio on the floor of our conservatory, and set to taking loads of pictures until I got the right ones.

Even though I took loads of photographs, it limited me in terms of design. The message needed to be clear and succinct, and for the 30 seconds you are sat reading it, it needs to be something that is going to stick. I came up with the tagline because I wanted it to be a powerful message. Yes, boobs can be sexy, but they are primarily feeders and can also be killers! That wasn't my tagline, I hadn't totally lost the plot. I was trying to get it printed and distributed in time for breast cancer awareness month and was hoping for some press to support it. I made a joke about going on This Morning a few times on my blog, but Phil and Holly ignored me. How rude. I still joke about it, and one day I will get on that sofa and raise awareness by sharing my story.

Back to the poster. I'm no graphic designer, but I was really pleased with my attempt and felt it was everything it needed it to be. Getting the message out, like I said, was harder because as soon as we put the posters up, they were taken down. My mum and I would sneak around nipping in toilets to put them up, as I had stopped asking businesses. It was disheartening being told it was against policy, time and time again, so we stopped being polite. I was like Booby Banksy, but without the spray paint and disguise, and I was actually still really lacking in confidence by this point and wasn't in a positive mind-set to push this further with companies. I think I was too scared of rejection because I hadn't yet processed what I'd been enduring. It was still so very personal and raw.

That month I went to a charity event that the breast unit hold annually and although I wasn't really myself, I enjoyed it, to a point. I didn't really like being part of the 'cancer club', with my pixie crop and lob sided boobs, not that anyone else knew that, but I was still too vulnerable and unsure of myself. It was clear this had knocked me for six and I'm sure no one really knew how I was feeling as I hid at home, most of the time over thinking things. I was planning so many things in my head, but I didn't have the brainpower to even write or organise my thoughts in any other way than this unrealistic and chaotic jumble.

That night I came face to face with a charity that had been recommended to me to support me through my journey. They were nice, normal, a few fellow pixie ladies in there, so I was brave and had a chat to them. I explained I'd avoided making contact until now as I didn't want to talk about cancer all the time, I didn't want it to define me. And that was understood. Neither did most of the women involved, to the point where it defined them, but it was the common denominator, wasn't it? It was bound to be the main initial focus, but the group was about empowering people to overcome and move forward. Something I was very keen to do. If someone had told me then, that I would go away for a weekend with a support group, I'd have run the other way. Back then, I knew the support was there, and I was more than comfortable with it being at arm's length. I don't think support groups are for everyone, but it's good to know you have that back up, even if it's just being able to make contact through social media, which was mostly what I needed.

My 15 Minutes of Fame

"In the future everyone will be famous for 15 minutes" Andy Warhol.

Me? In the news? A local journalist who had seen my blog and asked to cover the wedding and my blog, contacted me as part of a story. It turned out to be on the front page of our local rag, which caused some amusement to us. Some pupils we taught didn't even realise we were together until they saw us on the front page of the paper. Following this, our story was featured in the Liverpool Echo, Daily Mirror, Metro and on the Mail online site. I can't say I was totally comfortable with this national media coverage, but it was such a powerful way to share the message and raise awareness. I guess this meant compromising my privacy, but I suppose I had already signed this away by blogging on Facebook. The coverage led to a few very surreal messages. One which led to me being featured in Take a Break magazine a few months later but the 'Today' enquiry from America came to nothing. I was also contacted by someone in Australia. Whilst it was positive that this story was raising awareness, it was also scary, as it was easy to see how news and reporting escalates and can get out of hand quickly. Fortunately for me, it was all positive, although I had to get the Daily Mail to correct a few details, like my age (33 sounds better than 43 but hey) and another mistake that we had been together for 5 years! Not only hadn't we known each other 5 years previously, but we were also married to other people. You can see how people get into trouble.

Hi Sarah

I hope you don't mind me getting in touch like this, but I saw your story and wanted to say hello. What an amazing story and how brave that you've spoken out about what you're going through. Really is very inspirational. I work at a press agency called SWNS and write for the UK national magazines like Closer, Reveal, Woman, Bella, Take a Break and loads more. I was wondering how you would feel about sharing the story as a feature in one of the magazines? The article could express anything you wish and it might be a great way to share your experiences with a wider audience and the magazines do pay for your time. Feel free to message me over here or drop me a call.

Best wishes, Hattiexxx

Hi Sarah, I'm a reporter for TODAY.com in New York looking for a little info on you for a possible story pitch. Did you share the photo of you in your wedding gown and with a bald head as a way to encourage people to check for breast lumps?

Still no 'This Morning' sofa. "Why didn't they want me?" I asked myself. I didn't, really. I'm not stupid. I'm just not interesting enough, just one of hundreds, if not thousands, trying to raise awareness but, one day I will get there and I will raise awareness on a much bigger scale than I am now. Watch this space!

I'm told a personal story is much more effective than an NHS cancer campaign. I know all too well that people switch off and will not face their fears. Be it going for tests or self-examinations. I agree it can be scary, but it comes to a point where it will not go away, and avoidance only gives possible cancers more time to grow and become advanced. I've said it before, and I'll say it again. Check, share and stay aware. If in doubt, check it out. Yes, you!

Checks save lives

By Kelsey Maxwell
kelsey.maxwell@nqnw.co.uk

A BRIDE who was diagnosed with breast cancer last month shared a picture of her shaved head on her wedding day as a way of encouraging others to check themselves for lumps.

Sarah Vaughan, from Eccleston, was due to get married to fiance Rob in spring but after her diagnosis on December 7, the couple brought the date forward.

They tied the knot at St Helens Town Hall and held their reception at Saints on Saturday, January 6.

Two days before the ceremony, Sarah's hair started to fall out due to her chemotherapy.

And so the courageous mum-of-two shaved off her long locks and shared a picture her bald head online.

The image was placed by a Sarah, who is a teacher, on a Facebook page she set up to encourage women and men to check themselves every month.

The 43-year-old told the Star: "My hair started to come out last week so I decided to shave it and I got a wig for the big day.

"But I thought I would share the picture because I know many people may be scared to get lumps checked."

Sarah added: "I feel positive about my diagnosis.

"I thought I was good on checking myself and have had lumps checked out in the past that were nothing – but this time I must have missed it.

"The response to my page has been great, with some people messaging me saying they have found lumps and are getting them checked already – which is amazing."

The Facebook page called 'First of the month check for a lump,' has gained 430 followers within a week.

According to Cancer Research UK, more than one in 10 breast cancer cases are diagnosed late.

One in eight women and one in 870 men are diagnosed with breast cancer

Sarah and her husband Rob on their wedding day at Saints and (inset) the selfie she shared on Facebook

during their lifetime.

Breast and prostate cancer are also the most common cancers diagnosed in the UK

Sarah added: "This isn't for just women, everyone can get lumps and could save your life."

"But please if you find one get it checked and check yourselves every month – it could save your life."

Sarah is currently waiting for MRI results which will establish what stage the cancer is at.

To follow Sarah's page

visit firstofthemonththecheck-foralump on Facebook.

To share your story email news@sthelensstar.co.uk or contact our team via Facebook.

Son's book inspires cancer survivor mum

By Kelsey Maxwell

kelsey.maxwell@nqnw.co.uk

A CANCER survivor has made an video book based on popular children's book We Are Going on a Bear Hunt to encourage other people to check for lumps.

Sarah Vaughan, from Eccleston, thought she was good at checking her breasts for lumps, so she was shocked when she was diagnosed with breast cancer on December 7 2017. After five months of gruelling treatment, including chemotherapy, a mastectomy and reconstruction, she received the amazing news in June 2018 that she is now cancer free.

During her fight with the disease, the 45-year-old set up a Facebook page called @firstofthemonthcheckforalump to encourage women and men to check themselves on the first of every month. She has posted pictures using fruit to highlight what signs to check for, and the page has garnered 1,400 followers.

However, to mark two years

We're Going on a Boob Hunt.
A Parody by Sarah Vaughan!

Written and Illustrated by
Sarah Vaughan.

In conjunction with @firstofthemonthcheckforalump

since her diagnosis, the mum-of-four decided to pull together a video book called We Are Going on a Boob Hunt, based on children's book We Are Going on a Bear Hunt to raise more awareness of checking for lumps.

She said: "I was reading it to my five-year-old son Damian and thought it would be good to follow the pace of it and write a parody but to raise awareness of checking for lumps.

"It took a few months to sort it out, and I did the illustrations myself. My family asked whose voice it was, but it's mine!

"On December 8 it's two years since my initial diagnosis, and I wanted to show that yes the word cancer is really scary, but with early detection there is so much they can do to treat cancer.

"I want to use what happened to me to help others, and also put some humour

The front cover of her video book called We Are Going on a Boob Hunt. The video book is available to view on her Facebook page called First of the month check for a lump and at bit.ly/2Yh4wxG

Sarah is now doing well

into it.

"It's about making it memorable and repetitive so it gets into people's heads and they will remember to check and realise how easy it really is.

"If one person remembers and checks themselves and gets checked out earlier then that's what matters.."

■ To watch the video go to bit.ly/2Yh4wxG

Cancer survivor's poster promotes breast checks

By Kelsey Maxwell

news@sthelensstar.co.uk

A CANCER survivor has made a unique poster highlighting some of the potential symptoms of breast cancer as a way of encouraging others to check themselves for lumps this month.

Sarah Vaughan, from Eccleston, thought she was good at checking her breasts for lumps, so she was shocked when she was diagnosed with breast cancer on December 7. After five months of gruelling treatment including, chemotherapy, hair loss, mastectomy and reconstruction, she received the amazing news in June that she is now cancer free.

Despite fighting cancer, mum-of-two Sarah, set up a Facebook page to encourage women and men to check themselves on the first of every month. So to mark Breast Cancer Awareness Month, this

Sarah, with husband Rob, above, made this poster, right, urging others to check their breasts

October, she has designed a poster using grapefruits to show the signs of breast cancer – with the aim of putting these across the town centre on the back of doors in toilets and public bathrooms.

The 44-year-old told the Star: "I took the photos myself, I wanted to take

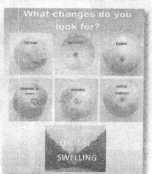

What changes do you look for?

TEXTURE   PUCKERING   LUMPS

CHANGES TO SHAPE   REDNESS   NIPPLE CHANGES

OR JUST SWELLING

a picture of melons originally, but they were all too perfect, and the next row up in Aldi had grapefruits,

which worked out really well. I thought I was good at checking for lumps on my breasts, but I ended

up with breast cancer, and through all of this I realise that lumps aren't the only sign of the disease. Boobs to some people aren't something they pay a lot of attention too, it's something to look good, so if they see a change in the mirror or they feel different, it's important they know that is a sign of it too. I think that by having something visual people can look at, maybe while they are sat on the toilet, they could check or think about it, rather than just information that won't stick. Many times a lump could be a cyst or benign, but not checking could potentially be life changing.

"I hope everyone takes these posters on board. I'm proud of them, and I hope they can prevent others going through what I have."

■ To follow Sarah's page visit firstofthemonthcheckforalump on Facebook. For more on the signs and symptoms go to breastcancercare.org.uk.

So, life goes on

So, I've said before, that people will surprise you when you have cancer, or life-changing events. Some will shock you by their absence; some will shock you by their presence in your life. I don't mean knocking on your door every day with a lasagne or cottage pie, I'm talking about the little things. The odd text or card in the post that arrives just when you need a pick me up. Offering to look after one of the kids or get you something when they are popping to the shops.

My friend and nail technician offered to do my nails for free. It was such a treat to have this pamper again as my nails were shocking by now and I'd neglected them. I'd gone to Sam for a while and she didn't have to offer, but she recognised it was something I might need after chemo and she wanted me to feel better about myself. It was a lovely gesture, and it felt so different, even just to have Shellac on my nails.

It was just in time for a special night out too. I was wedding reception ready and looking forward to seeing my friends from the running group I'd been avoiding, due to lack of confidence. It was weird going out again and trying to be normal when I didn't really know what to talk about, as all I'd been doing was recovering from cancer and I struggled to know how to relate to people. However, a few gins certainly helped with that.

On the dance floor, I was so overwhelmed with happiness at being back with my friends and perplexed by how I'd convinced myself to avoid them and I cried. I wasn't sad. I didn't recognise this new feeling that I now know was joy! It felt euphoric, and I liked it. It gave me a new lease of life, if that is not too clichéd, and brought me back to what I'd been missing. I knew it was time to face up to getting back to my 'new normal' and I needed to be around people.

I had a few issues before I could plan on going back to work. I still had to have six more Herceptin injections every three weeks. At that point in my treatment, I would take ages to wake up in the morning; it was like they were injecting me with sixty percent teenager and forty percent pensioner, as I was walking around like CP30 in the morning, until my joints warmed up. I would also get spasms and tingles and electric shocks around my elbow and down to my hands, which were getting me down. Sometimes though I wondered if I was imagining it, as when I didn't get it, I couldn't imagine the feeling, if that makes any sense at all.

I was also still needing my 'nana nap'. I would put the fire on after lunch and watch one of those murder programmes on 'ID'. The type that repeats the same murder scene shot every ten seconds and tells you the same information after every advert just in case you missed it the previous thirty-six times before. The type of American TV shit where you don't have to think. Then I'd feel bad that poor Kathleen in Chester County, Idaho, was brutally murdered, left naked in a ditch, and I was now using her death for light entertainment to get me to sleep on a wet and windy Wednesday afternoon. Maybe it was time to go back to work...

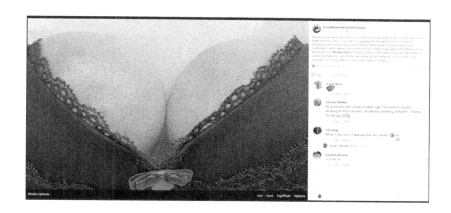

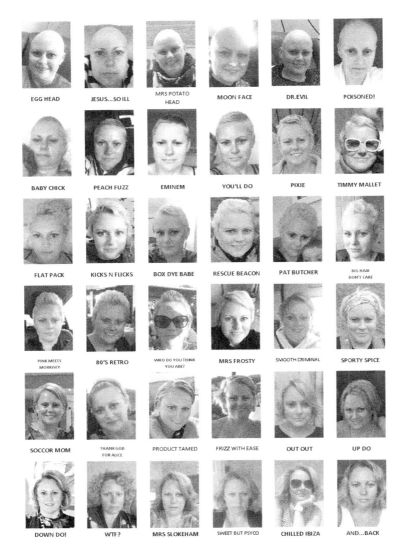

EGG HEAD

JESUS...SO ILL

MRS POTATO HEAD

MOON FACE

DR.EVIL

POISONED!

BABY CHICK

PEACH FUZZ

EMINEM

YOU'LL DO

PIXIE

TIMMY MALLET

FLAT PACK

KICKS N FLICKS

BOX DYE BABE

RESCUE BEACON

PAT BUTCHER

BIG HAIR DON'T CARE

PINK MEETS MORRISEY

80'S RETRO

WHO DO YOU THINK YOU ARE?

MRS FROSTY

SMOOTH CRIMINAL

SPORTY SPICE

SOCCOR MOM

THANK GOD FOR ALICE

PRODUCT TAMED

FRIZZ WITH EASE

OUT OUT

UP DO

DOWN DO!

WTF?

MRS SLOKEHAM

SWEET BUT PSYCO

CHILLED IBIZA

AND...BACK

Gosh, Isn't your Hair Growing Fast

Actually, I think I really knew it was time to go back, when one day I found the energy to clean the oven. It was bloody sparkling. Unlike me, who was morphing into a Pat Butcher look alike.

I don't mean I was wearing three-inch-long earrings to clean the cooker and shouting "Frank", but Lord only knows what was happening to my hair. It was growing up and out and scaring the life out of my family. The bigger it got, the more I bleached it. Suddenly it wouldn't comb flat anymore and if it rained, then no one for a mile would get wet as it looked like a large mushroom.

Losing your hair can be traumatic and so symbolic of cancer and chemo. But no one prepared me for the perils of this crazy mop growing back and doing what it wanted. From shaving the first few fluffy chick-like growths, to first dye-ing it, and looking like Eminem. It was a tricky process working through the metamorphosis of re-growth. Chemo damages the follicles and makes them kink, so the first hair growth is usually curly and frizzy. Add that to my Brian May locks and you could see me coming a mile away. It really took some taming. A little part of me won't lie. I hoped it might come back sleek, straight and soft. You know, like Gwyneth Paltrow before she went all Goop! Alas, no - sleek it was not.

I was so impatient to look like me again. Totally over the novelty of being bald, and not having to wash my hair, style it, pay for highlights etc. but too impatient to wait until the six months post chemo to get my colour done. I hated the salt and pepper look. It might have worked for Philip Schofield, but it didn't work for me. I looked like my brother (no offence to him, but he's a man). I wanted to look feminine; I wanted to be blond again, and I wanted it to be long enough not to spring up like Marge Simpson.

I thought I'd give you a good laugh and compile the pictures of regrowth so you could see what I had to contend with. Check out my work badge... I thought this looked good at the time... God, help me! So, when someone looked at me and said, "Gosh! Isn't your hair growing?" I think what they had missed at the end of that was 'up and out'.

Everyone commented on my hair. I guess it's a relief for people to see hair growth as a sign of good health, well, better health. It's hard to lose your hair and then see it grow back and still not feel like yourself. But ultimately, I think it's a big part of you that singles you out as the chemo patient, and that's awkward for people to see, especially as it made me look really sick and I didn't have hair to hide behind. I'm sure it's easier to comment on your barnet than for folks to say. "How are you, now you've not died?" People rarely have the words to communicate what they really want to say or ask, but what they really want to know is... has your treatment worked? Will you survive? We are so very British and will comment on what we see has changed rather than go in for the kill but, no one will come out and refer to your mortality, as this is taboo.

144

More Hair than Brian

That last school day before Christmas, when everyone was hyper, was my first day back after a year off and I was most certainly dazed and confused. I got little 'work' done, but I could meet new kids on a more informal basis, familiarise myself with the place again and reorganise a few things. I'd been off more than a year and I didn't know where to start in getting things back to where I wanted them. I am very particular about my classroom and resources, and it was like starting again. It wasn't trashed by any means. My replacements (there had been three) had done a good job it was just they worked differently to me, and let's just say, I'm a bit 'Monica from Friends' about my 'stuff'. Someone once commented that if they stood around long enough in my classroom, I'd label them. What's not to like about that? I like things organised.

Returning then meant I didn't spend the Christmas holidays worrying about it as I had taken the first step. Plus, it wasn't an immediate return. I still had three more weeks in January to increase my days back to four. My very generous phased return from the council!

What I found the most difficult about going back were that things had been erased from my 'marshmallow Brian' which is how I continued to spell brain. I'd forgotten names of people who I worked with. Not the immediate ones I was in contact with daily, but people from agencies and schools whom we dealt with. Acronyms in teaching are like petrol to a car and I'd forgotten some of those and processes for referrals etc. Helpfully, things change fast in education and procedures and protocols are always being tweaked and the wheel gets reinvented so much, I'm surprised it's still round.

Let's not mention passwords. Nowhere in my head had I made space to remember passwords. Who bloody invented them anyway? Never mind four hundred and seventy-five characters to include every pet's birthday or car registration you have ever had with a hash tag or asterisk, but not a forward slash. Your password has to be something you will never remember ever again as we need to keep your accounts secret from not just the FBI, the mafia, and the entire cast of 'Corrie', but from yourself. Because you must choose something so complicated, you won't even recognise it even if you wrote it down.

(MI5 please take note I would obviously never do this... God forbid)

Passwordzmyarse!# (note the capital P!) Shit no number... Passwordzmyarse44!#

Don't underestimate the adjustment to return to work after a serious illness, I was so exhausted in those first few months. It was enjoyable, and I felt purposeful in a way I hadn't for a while. I was good at my job and I had forgotten this. I know that's not very British of me, but it was nice to have some good feelings again, knowing I could do something well, and I think I'd lost sight of this along the way. I mean, that oven was sparkling, but it wasn't like the kids came in from school and shouted "Wow, look at that clean oven, Mum, you're amazing".

A positive element of nearly dying is I really struggled to be affected by a lot of issues that may have bothered me before. Some things in life are just not important, and whilst I was still dedicated and hardworking, I would not get wound up by things I couldn't change. I also realised how positive and philosophical I'd become. I was keen to continue referring to growth mind-set and resilience in a lot of my teaching too. I had really believed in what I was saying about changing negatives into positives, as I'd done it, with brilliant success, I'd say.

I believe many people re-evaluate their lives after an experience like this and change career and I can certainly see why. If I could have afforded to leave the profession after diagnosis, I would have done as I felt and still felt, I have so much to do and so little time to do it in. I could never be bored, but it was the right step to go back to my life before, as that was part of me and my identity, for now. I had big ideas for the future but had learnt that Rome wasn't built in a day. But like this book, chapter by chapter, it came together and so will my plans.

Firstofthemonthcheckforalump

1 January · G

Ive been writing this for a year now. Im hoping it works and you are in the habit of checking . Did you all check today? If not do it now!! Or put a date in your diary to do it some time this month depending on the best time for you. Promise me you won't just read this and then forget to check? Remember it's about looking for changes as well as feeling for them. Happy to say goodbye to 2018 but it wasn't all bad was it? I got a free boob job after all. Well half a boob job. Ok so not half a boob as that would be weird. Hoping that 2019 brings me boob job no 2. And some normality, whatever that means. Wishing you all a happy and healthy 2019. As usual check and share. Happy New year. Xx

👍❤️ Lauren Hill and 85 others   13 comments 21 shares

👍 Like   💬 Comment   ↗ Share

Boost Post

A New Year, and New start, a New me.... and I'm feeling... Bloody Shattered

Christmas 2018 was so much fun. I spent ages making the house lovely and decorating our table for Christmas lunch. As far as I was concerned, this was our first Christmas in the house. However, a Christmas day Nerf gun incident took me back to A&E, a year on from my last yuletide visit. I was going to be invited to their parties soon. The visit was brief. It wasn't my eye that had been temporarily blinded. Thankfully, and otherwise, Christmas passed by with lots of laughter, joy and family fun.

A New Year, a new start, a new me. But I was still feeling bloody shattered! Fatigue is a real, debilitating thing. But it was slowly getting stronger, day by day, and that I was thankful for. I was also thankful that I had been signed off by the oncologist for two whole years! This felt amazing. The trust you have in this stranger, who in-expectantly comes into your life, is something else. I guess you literally trust them with your life, don't you? That they one day have faith that your treatment is virtually over, and they no longer need to see you, is a big milestone. And I was thankful for their care.

I'd requested a Dexa scan (bone density scan), as I was worried about my body's inability to make Vitamin D and therefore this, and the treatment's effects on my bones, was a concern and sure enough I was diagnosed with Osteopenia. In layperson's terms it meant my bones were now more like 'Weetabix' but not yet 'Rice Crispy'. It wasn't a major concern right now, and they wanted to repeat the scan to check me in two years for deterioration, which with some calcium tablets, put my mind at rest. But otherwise, they didn't want or need to see me on a regular basis.

It was also monumental that I was to be stopping the Herceptin, as I'd come to the end of my year of treatment, and this felt fantastic. I didn't have massive life changing side effects from this targeted therapy, but it was something I was putting up with and I guess, if I'd had this first, with no other treatment, I may have noticed how tired it made me and how sore my joints were, but these were also the lasting effects of chemo, so just went with feeling a lot older than my years and was something I had come to terms with.

It was another massive box ticked to complete Herceptin, however, and it thrilled me to not have the thousand pounds of drugs pumped into my leg, from now on. I've said it before and I'll say it again - thank you, NHS. To have this in the first place was an honour, as it had been a postcode lottery treatment, at one point. To have it at home was a luxury and to be treated by lovely reassuring nurses, who really cared about my welfare, was so nice. It made an unpleasant experience so much less so because they took their time not to hurt me. Although there was one time, I woke up in the middle of the night, after one injection in pain and struggling to walk. I don't know why. Maybe it had slightly gone in and damaged a little nerve or something and was so painful. Thankfully it was short lived and with some pain relief I was fine.

We had also been married over a year now, and what a year it had been! If 'for better for worse' meant anything, it did that year. I had been so very lucky and to have Rob look after us all so well, is something I will always be grateful for. Now was the time to live and continue making memories for us and our families.

DO YOU HAVE THE BALLS
TO CHECK YOURS?

The signs of testicular cancer can be subtle or not always visible. After a warm bath or shower, take the testicle (and the tube that connects them) between your thumb and finger and roll around checking for lumps/fluid. Look for:

Change in texture or testicle becomes hard

Pain/heaviness in the testes or scrotum

Change in SIZE of a testicle.

A LUMP or enlargement in either testicle

- Other symptoms are a dull ache in the back or groin and breast tenderness.
- Get into the habit of checking on the first of every month and if in doubt, check it out.
- Your GP has seen it all and most lumps are not cancerous.
- Get to know your body and then you can spot any changes as around 2300 men are diagnosed in the UK every year.

#thumbyourplums

#firstofthemonthcheckforalump

153

Thumb your Plumbs

Being back at work didn't mean less campaigning. The passion to use my situation and experience to raise awareness was still fierce. These next few months I designed a poster for testicular cancer with the tagline 'Thumb your Plums' Testicular cancer isn't one of the biggest cancer killers, but men can be very good at ignoring health issues and avoiding getting checked out so to compliment the toilet door poster idea, I thought it was only fair to include them too. Really, I should have done a breast cancer poster for men, as although it is rare, 350 men a year will get breast cancer compared to 55,000 women per year, it is still a concern.

As I had included men in my campaign, I approached the local rugby league team, St. Helens (Saints), to see if they could promote my campaign. Kindly, they included a feature on my campaign in the match programme and they invited us as guests to the game. They also included my story that week through their social media, so I hope that quite a few people read my story and were inspired to check.

It wasn't the impact I'd wanted, because of having to omit the posters I'd designed. It was thought the frank messages would upset some fans. They had received complaints before and didn't want to risk upsetting anyone. I get people don't want the hassle, but this is a game where every time they score a try or goal, half naked teenage girls come out with their pom-poms and perform their kicks and flicks in front of a mainly older male demographic. But hey, don't thumb your plumbs to check for cancer... that would step way outside anyone's comfort zone. Cheer at the girls but don't check your 'nads'... and so no poster on the back of toilet doors, for fear of a backlash.

Really, I wanted to streak half naked onto the pitch and show the 'fuddy duddy's' my reconstructed 'pom-pom's' - put that in your pipe and bloody smoke it! But I respected the club was kind enough to give me a platform, and it wasn't their views but the possible views of a minority of fans. It's difficult, when campaigning, to come up against resistance. To me, having lived it, checking is so important, but it just doesn't feature on many people's radar and like I've mentioned before, plenty of folk are happy to bury their head because it will never happen to them. Denial is a genuine thing, and I get it. Cancer is scary!

I have to confess with all my health issues I'd ignored going for a smear and was two years overdue. How very self-righteous of me to raise awareness of breast cancer but ignore the fact that I'd put off my smear in the year before my diagnosis. I'd somehow convinced myself putting it off to the next month would be okay, so I know how much chipping away needs to be done to convince people to take responsibility for their health. Make of that what you will but when I was going through treatment, I'd mentioned it to the oncologist who said not to worry as any stray cells (if there were any) would be suitably zapped by the poison that was rippling through my body on any given day.

Alas, the time had come to pull my big girl knickers up (and down) and have a smear. I spoke to the lovely nurse about my avoidance

155

previously and explained that I'd been so sick of being poked and prodded from all the miscarriages.

I'd also had a really unpleasant experience once with a very rough nurse who had said she couldn't find my cervix and rummaged, elbow deep, to what felt like my sternum, in order to retrieve said cervix and take the swab. The nurse was cross at this revelation but professionally began the smear with a smaller (plastic) speculum and was done in seconds. Who bloody knew they didn't have to crank up your vagina with a cold metal massive car jack and shout at you if you weren't relaxed! It only took until 44 to work this out. "Lovely Nurse", where had you been when I was having, 'Dodgy Battle Axe Nurses', with hairy chins and B.O? Ok, so that's more of a Roald Dahl character, but you get my drift.

And this brings me to my results...you must buy book two to find this out!!! Only joking, I'm never writing a book again. Pleased to say it was negative, nothing lurking or suspicious for me (thank the bloody Lord), as I was all 'cancered' out.

FIRST OF THE MONTH CHECK FOR A LUMP.

I'd always thought I was good at checking for lumps until back in Dec '17 I was diagnosed with stage 3 breast cancer. I was shocked at the size of the lump and how I'd not noticed it develop. I then realised it was probably months not weeks since I had last checked. I suppose it's become complacent and had a 'this won't happen to me' attitude especially aged 43. I had a long road ahead of treatment and was almost kicking myself I hadn't been more vigilant. I wasn't alone after talking to friends who also admitted they rarely checked their breast for changes or lumps it prompted me to raise awareness through a thing called 'first of the month check for a lump' which I began on the 1st Jan 18. The idea behind it is that if you check on a set date every month it becomes a habit. Any change is that are indeed can be checked quickly by your GP as early detection for any cancer increases the survival rate dramatically. I learnt a lot in these first few weeks. 55,000 women will receive a breast cancer diagnosis each year. Breast cancer can present as visual changes not just lumps and guess what men can also develop breast cancer although it's around 300 a year.

So between chemo, getting married with a wig on and trying to remain sane, I got into the habit of posting on the 1st of every month to remind people when and how to check. It became a bit of a diary as I went throughout 6 rounds of gruelling chemo, surgery and then radiotherapy and although I brought dark humour and bared my soul to the blog it quickly became apparent that I was helping people and turning this negative experience into a positive. I received many personal messages thanking me for raising awareness as they too had found a lump or noticed a visual change and are now being treated with a good prognosis from early detection. A really good friend had found a lump in his testicle and was about to be treated for testicular cancer. He said he never would have checked if it had not been for my campaign. Recently I have designed two posters for the back of toilet doors to raise awareness of Breast cancer and Testicular cancer.

We're hoping that seeing this article can prompt people to get into the habit of checking every month. This is what you should look out for:

Breast cancer - Feel For Lumps, Save Your Bumps.

- A lump in the breast or armpit
- Dimpling or changes in skin texture
- Inverted or weeping nipple
- Redness/inflammation
- Changes to size and shape

Testicular cancer - Use your thumbs to check your plums.

- A lump or enlargement in the testicle
- Changes to size or shape
- Heaviness/pain in the testicle
- Change in texture or the testicle becomes hard
- A dull ache in the back or groin

157

 **Firstofthemonthcheckforalump**

1 May · 🌐

Happy First of the month everyone. Did you check today? I went one better and had a mammogram. (Only one boob because the reconstructed one has no breast tissue in it) Over quick and painless but my first one since treatment. I'm not worrying about it, what's the point? So don't be scared to check today. Look for changes in the mirror as well as feeling for changes. If in doubt get referred by your GP. I'm writing this Sat in the hospital as I'm having a pre op today too. My 'boob job' is at the end of May where the fantastic plastic surgeon will even me out and make me look fabulous (hopefully) he's already refused me a bit of Lipo though. 😩😩 at least I'll need a hairnet for this op😷 I'm currently doing my best Madonna true blue hairstyle but woke up more like sideshow Bob. To be fair I'm more Bob than Madge but who cares, im alive and kicking and ready to walk the three peaks on Sat and Sunday. If you have a fiver to spare I'm including the link here but no pressure as I know every day people are doing sponsored stuff. Have a happy day and please please share to get the message out. Much love Madonna 😊xxxx

https://uk.virginmoneygiving.com/3peakssarahvaughan

👍😍 Joan Jacobson and 45 others   5 comments 24 shares

Ain't no mountain High Enough

I think I had something to prove to myself by doing another physical challenge, and a marathon was not an option. It was too isolating to do the training, too much time away from the family, and it was not something that appealed to me at that time. Luckily for me, my running group announced the Three Peaks Challenge, and I thought, "Yeah! I can manage that"! It was the 'Three Peaks (Ben Nevis, Scafell Pike and Snowdon), not quite in 24-hours, but as quickly as we could manage safely. And so, the training began. This time I'd encouraged Rob to join us. We did some walks together as a sizeable group and we did some walks together as a family. It was clear quite early on; this wasn't just walking up a few hills. If surviving cancer taught me anything, it was I can do this. I was determined as ever.

On one of the training walks up Helvellyn, we found ourselves in really dangerous weather conditions at the top. We were caught in a blizzard and huddled together like penguins, slipping, sliding, falling and freezing. I'm not sure what we expected as we were told time and time again that this challenge was going to be tough. A few people dropped out after this, but it didn't put many of us off as we would go up these mountains in early summer, so the conditions would be pleasant. Next time, I will listen carefully to my auntie, who has over fifty years' experience volunteering in Langdale and Ambleside mountain rescue. Not that we weren't prepared, we weren't stupid! But the weather does turn, and it is something to be respected, as we learnt. We'd encouraged our 11-year-old to join us on some training walks and he'd then signed up for the challenge, which as responsible parents, would not have happened, if we thought there were tremendous risks. Plus, it was great to bond with him and he was like a mountain goat and certainly fearless.

We got up at 4am that Saturday morning in early May and over 40 of us met up to begin our adventure. It was exciting setting out in tandem. Three minibuses and our food van to drive to our first mountain, Ben Nevis. Our spirits were high. If I tell you that the name Ben Nevis translates into 'venomous mountain' you may know what is coming next.

I can honestly say descending that mountain was one of the most horrendous experiences that I've ever had. It was tough at the top. Visibility was low, -15 degrees was the temperature, but we were excited as we had done the hardest part, we just had to come down now and what could be harder than going up? I don't know what possessed me, but I took my gloves off at the top to eat a sandwich and didn't put them back on straight away as we were taking pictures at the summit and stayed up there for way too long. After about 5-minutes descending, we got lost and separated from the rest of our group. Suddenly the landscape was like Mars (not that I've ever been). I felt pain in my fingers and hands. It was excruciating, debilitating, but almost at the same time it felt like they had fallen off. I then became exhausted and just wanted to stop and sit down. I felt sick, disorientated and wanted to curl up and go to sleep.

After about an hour of walking in virtual silence, as I struggled to string a sentence together, I realised I would have to give up the challenge, and I was so upset. I was too tired and numb to cry and just kept asking to stop and rest, but rightly so they wouldn't let me. The descent went on and on; I felt like I was letting them down. With my heavy legs, I felt I was dragged down those hills. Every corner walked, it felt we were nearly there, but it was round another one, then another one, and the light was fading. But I was improving. I decided there and then that this was much harder than running a marathon, as a marathon seemed to have an endpoint and lots of cheering supporters all the way. Eventually, we managed just before dusk, to get back to the buses and the food van. I nearly cried.

I had the most amazing cup of Heinz Tomato Soup that felt like a blood transfusion, and within about thirty minutes I was back feeling more like me again. Although exhausted, there was relief as I knew I would be ok to climb the other two mountains. I don't quite know if I had a slight hypothermia or altitude sickness when I was at the top but feeling better at the bottom was like magic and I was so thankful.

I'm sharing this story because it felt like I'd hit rock bottom (no pun intended) when I was having chemo but somewhere, I got the strength to do that little bit more, and get through it, and this is what this experience felt like. We can always dig deep and climb our way out (or down), when needed. I have that in me and so do you. You just may not have been pushed there yet. Resilience is so important and something we should teach our children. It's difficult, when faced with a challenge, to crack on and not give up, but people are doing it all the time because the alternative isn't an option, is it? So, going back to the start of this book, and my quote by Elizabeth Edwards... "She stood in the storm and when the wind did not blow her way, she adjusted her sails".

We all have to adjust our sails sometimes and often when we least expect it.

Firstofthemonthcheckforalump
3 June at 14:12 · 🌐   ···

There is a reason I'm two days late posting this month. I'm currently in Hotel Whiston waiting for my boob job and thought it was more apt to post now. I'm so glad it's eventually happening as I've had a few dates now but I'm here.... hoping to get to theatre before 5 but who knows. I've been drawn on but I'm worried that the Sharpie is coming off and they will put the nipple in the wrong place as I do have another dot drawn on my neck. 😵 ha could you imagine....At least I'd get in Take a Break again! Also I'm thrilled to see I have a hair net with my gown awaiting adornment....most fetching I know but a year on I'm glad I have hair to put in it. So posting two days late is a good test. Did you check?? If not then please do. Type 'done' and please share the post. Thrilled to say my mammogram was clear. Not thrilled to say I'm nil by mouth😩 got no dinner but I have got a Zimmer! Xx

👍😊❤ Rebecca Twist and 152 others   67 comments 29 shares

👍 Like   💬 Comment   ↪ Share

Under the knife again (Boob Job Two)

My second boob job was cancelled (I bet Katie Price never had that problem) and I was totally gutted. Not only was I looking forward to a shiny new nipple and an uplift, but I had also spent weeks in work setting up for my summer absence, the supply teacher was booked at work and I was ready to handover, having got everything up-to-date and primed my classes. I now had all the childcare sorted. Who was looking after whom and when, which is no mean feat! I was mentally psyched up, but mostly; I wanted a bit more of a normal body back.

I'm not somebody who obsesses about the way I look but I'm no spring chicken and whilst my 'Toob' was firm and pert, my natural boob was by now rubbing on my waistband and just like my spirits, needed a lift.

After my initial upset, I was proactive, and I knew that obviously I wasn't a priority, as it was cosmetic, not life threatening, I rang my surgeon's secretary and asked if there was anything that could be done. I figured there was no point brooding. I couldn't change the fact it had been cancelled, but I could try to influence the date of my next surgery, hopefully.

Luckily, my polite persistence paid off, and I was booked in for a few days later, as they worked out, I could be slotted in after a Diep reconstruction. Not sure how comfortable I was with knowing the surgeons would have operated for twelve hours and would then work on me, but I couldn't face months and months more waiting with the risk of cancellation, so I immediately agreed and was booked in.

I arrived at 'Hotel Whiston' a few days later than planned, bright and early but preparing to wait around all day. And that I did. They admitted me for surgery around five pm. It went well, and I was home the next day with porn-star swollen bosoms hiding under layered dressings. I was so exhausted, but it had gone well so recovery could now begin.

What they had cleverly done was some nipple sharing from my real boob onto the tummy boob, to recreate an areola. I had enough to remove some of it and stitch onto my toob, think applique but with skin! With the cartilage they had removed from my rib, and stored under my toob during the mastectomy, he created an actual nipple by sewing it to the bit of my stomach skin that now sat on my toob. I had liposuction to remove some stomach tissue under my armpit, which felt like a hard side boob, and I also had an uplift to hitch up my droopy boob from my waistband.

It was clever surgery, and he made for a fine sculptor that evening. Oh, and talking of waistbands, he had cut off the dog ear excess from the end of my Diep scar. I looked like a bit of a patchwork quilt but that was ok, it would heal and mend, and I was confident I would be right as rain soon enough.

I'd forgotten about my reaction to the adhesive on the dressings, which causes a burning rash and becomes so irritable, matching my mood post-surgery. If you've had stitches, you'll know the itchy tightness around the wound as the skin heals and knits together and brings the little insomnia fairies out to play. Yes, I had also forgotten how difficult it was to sleep when recovering and remained propped up for what felt like months.

I was exhausted and struggled to get a decent night's sleep, which delayed my return to work. I was having such crazy dreams and I remember writing this down with a list for the surgeon, (yes, I'm that nightmare patient) who laughed at my thorough list of questions. I'm not sure he had much sympathy for my lack of sleep as who knows when he actually sleeps because he spends most of his life in theatres performing to his comatose crowd.

I'd not asked him about the pens we had gifted him, but I presumed he still had them, and he'd not downgraded his pencil case back to a sandwich bag. I was more concerned for my new nipple; it was huge! I had a lovely polystyrene polo mint frame to protect my Malteser-sized nip. This was to prevent it being squashed whilst it was healing and I was expected to recreate my own, with gauze, for up to six weeks. This, and the attractive compression socks, meant the recovery process dragged, and I was disappointed the healing on my uplift was very slow underneath. The weight of my boobs just pulled on the stitches and they took ages to heal.

This all paled into significance as I'd had brilliant news. It was much more important than the surgery and slow healing. The news that my first mammogram was clear of cancer! What an amazing feeling and relief this was. The fear stays with you daily, that cancer could return, but for now, this was my good health news top-up for a while, and I loved it. Things were looking good, and these were all steps closer back to finding me again.

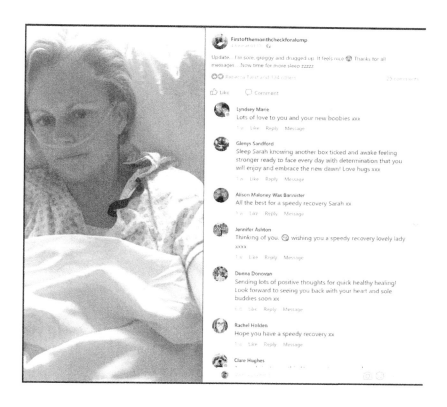

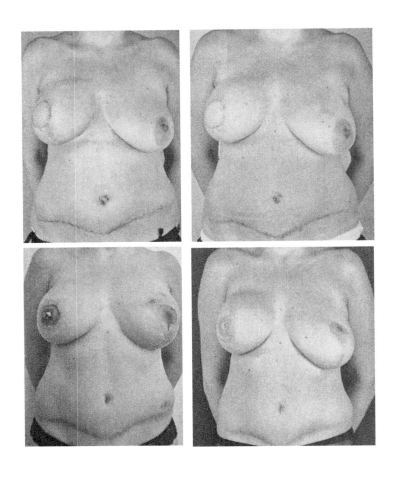

168

Breast of Nope and Gory

I've shared these images and medical photographs for a few reasons. Please view them with respect, as this wasn't a simple decision. However, these photographs don't define me. They visually describe my surgery and how my body has changed through breast cancer. If they offend you, then skip this chapter. I'm sharing them to dispel myths and stem the fear. It's impossible to find images on the internet that tell an authentic story, but why shouldn't I share what I've been through? And importantly, I'm proud of the way I look now, and I'm not embarrassed by a few scars. I want people to see how amazing the outcomes can be from mastectomy and reconstruction. I want to take away some horror because when you have the unknown, you fill in the blanks.

I'm proud of my body. Scars, lumps, bumps, rolls, it's me, it's mine, and it's real. Nobody looks photoshopped when they look in the mirror. Most of us hate our bodies or something about our reflection, and we put too much pressure on ourselves to look a certain way. Have you ever looked back at photographs of yourself and thought, "I wish I looked that slim/tanned/pert now?" However, at the time you want to be slimmer, more tanned, pert and taught. Why do we do this to ourselves?

In fact, I've often thought. "What if we spoke to each other the way we speak to ourselves? We would have no friends, would we?" I'm not sharing these images to shock. I'm not sharing them to get attention. I just feel that there needs to be more honesty.

These pictures are filter and Photoshop free. I know the stitches and infection aren't nice to look at if you're squeamish, but it's important to see healing and not sugar-coat anything. But how amazing are our bodies? We can be sliced and diced, yet we recover and move forward and I'm very thankful for that. Let's not forget the amazing skill set that the NHS provides us with. My surgeon was a keen artist who decided he could put that creativity to good use and go into plastic surgery. Although it's not 'Turner prize' quality yet, he's getting there! I'm still due further surgery to correct a few more things. As you can see, the uplift hasn't been as successful, so a different technique is to be used, allowing my heavy boob to withstand the lift this time. I think he wants to experiment with the cartilage that has created my nipple too. If this works, I will then be offered some tattooing to finish the process.

I feel really lucky to have the chance to have an immediate reconstruction as not everyone can, and I know some have had to deal with huge physical reminders of their cancer, whilst having to wait. It's not for everybody, but I'd never considered not having a new boob, and I think the surgeons have done a superb job. I hope you take from this something positive and you're not repulsed. I guess if you are the issues lie with your perception of beauty and not mine, but that's for a different book!

171

Cancer Weekender

So, as I had mentioned before, I had become a member of a cancer support group, even though I was reluctant to do this. I didn't really want to identify as someone who had had cancer and that be the only thing that labelled me; however, I was trying to be more open-minded and when invited away for a therapy type weekend; I agreed. What did I have to lose? Some time for me to reflect and meet new people could only be a good thing, Couldn't it?

As the Wales trip drew closer, I realised I wasn't really feeling it. I only really knew one other person, and she was as apprehensive as me.

I'm ashamed to say that when we arrived at our meeting place, I wondered what the hell I'd got myself into. The nerves took over, and I was already planning my escape as I had family who could pick me up as they lived close by. The journey was fine, and on arrival the place looked amazing, but as I dragged my case up the stairs that feeling of dread was still with me and the negativity crept in.

These are not my people.

I don't want to sit and mope about cancer.

I don't want to drag the past two years up.

I don't want to do crafts or paint by numbers.

Yep, I was negative and grumpy, but actually on reflection; I think it scared me. Scared to face what I'd been through because I was getting on with life. I didn't need that s**t dragging up as I was way ahead of the game and had moved on. When we all got together for our first task, I painted on a smile and I tried to remain positive. We had a little induction but then were thrown into our first activity. It was hide and bloody seek! I cannot tell you how much fun it was reverting to such a childhood favourite and what a way to break the ice. We laughed, and we screamed as we ran and hid from each other, and it felt ridiculous. We didn't even know each other's names at that point, but it didn't matter. It was cleverly done to relax us and that it did. Even claustrophobic old me, hid in a dark wardrobe trying not to give the game away.

What followed that weekend was really special. Did we talk about cancer? Hell yeah! We also did the odd craft activity, and the snobby art teacher in me really enjoyed it. I found it therapeutic and meaningful and it was a process rather than a polished, gallery-worthy finished piece. Structured time and activities were included but gave way to some real understanding of what we've all been through. It wasn't easy, but the one thing we all had in common was cancer. When we got off that bus and dragged our suitcases up the hill, we all had cancer in common. But we left having laughed hard and drank plenty, all whilst reflecting on our shared experiences and it was comforting.

We compared our cancer war wounds in the kitchen at 11 p.m. after a few gins. We drank fizz in the hot tub at three am and friendships were made, as we sat chatting and drinking in the rain, as cheesy as it sounds. I'm most definitely ashamed of myself now for judging how I thought the weekend would go when I first got there.

What I took away with me was that it's ok to feel vulnerable, it's ok to reflect, it's ok to cry and not have to put a brave face on all the time. I realised that no matter what is thrown at you, there are always people there for you, who can support you in so many ways. It takes time to work out who they are and what you want or need from them. I think therefore it's so hard to support someone through cancer. I would say just be there. Be present for them, ask and suggest. If they are not forthcoming in asking for support, then just do. Thank you to the people in my life who just did. Thank you to the people who came away on that weekend who allowed me to be me. You all know who you are.

Sunday Bloody Sunday, And Monday and Tuesday and Wednesday

A brilliant side effect of chemo, for me personally, was infertility. I never thought I'd say infertility would be a good thing, after everything I'd been through, but was at a stage where I was more than happy to stop having periods. I'd got to the summer being period free for 18 months and was pretty convinced, because of the hot flushes, and lack of menses, that I was menopausal. Bring on the 'change'!

Summer 2019 brought our lovely holiday to Montenegro. It was the night where my skin was bronze and shimmery, that I'd put on my white linen dress for the evening entertainment, as I rocked that holiday glow. Yes, that white dress night was the night my period made a surprise appearance. F**k! Why me? Why now? The Goddess of menstruation was not on my side that night. Why, oh why, did they choose the white dress at night?

I guess it was better than arriving when in my bikini around the pool. I mean, I hadn't brought tampons on holiday. I thought I was home and dry? What the hell is applicator in Montenegrin? I never found out; poor Rob did that shopping trip! Having been pissed off, I hoped it was the last hurrah, as I certainly didn't want to have to go through the menopause again.

I tried not to let it get me down and enjoyed the rest of the holiday. We returned home, but the days bled into weeks and the bleeding became heavier and heavier, to where I worried that something was terribly wrong. The 'cancer gremlins' rearing their ugly heads again. I ignored my advice and Dr Google led me down the path of catastrophising about the plausible reasons why I couldn't get off the loo without flooding.

The GP wasn't concerned and prescribed me Northisterone, a wonder drug that stops bleeding, but it took up to a week for the bleeding to stop. I'd just finished my 10-day course, and the bleeding returned with a vengeance and excuse the pun, was such a pain in the arse as it was too heavy to get on with normal life. By now we were into the new term, but thankfully the toilet in work is opposite my classroom. Some might say my 'en-suite', but this still didn't make it less of a nuisance.

By now, they had sent me for tests and a hysteroscopy where a camera is inserted into your womb and they scrape the lining to test the cells (don't worry, the gas and air was bloody lovely). Thankfully, I was given another dose of Northisterone and sent on my way. I was diagnosed with dysfunctional uterine bleeding which needed monitoring but did not need treatment as they would check in six months if the womb lining had changed. However, the bleeding escalated and one evening I called 111 from the toilet that I had spent all night on, continuously bleeding.

So, this being me, they obviously felt I'd been away too long and sent me on a trip to A&E as the blood loss was too excessive. Sad to say, what awaited was carnage. Beds everywhere in the corridors and people were really sick, which made me feel guilty as I was sure I just needed some pills and maybe a couple of units of vintage red and I could go back to the loo at home.

They placed me in what I can only describe really, as a medical cupboard, without knowing for sure, but thankfully it was next to the toilet which I made full use of. I was sent for blood tests, not knowing that I would not walk out of that room, but I would wind up being dramatically whizzed into resus because of passing out, as she couldn't get blood from me (the irony).

After four hours being closely monitored, they sent me off to a ward for the night so I could sleep, and they could monitor me. I should point out, at this stage, the reason they had panicked when I fainted was because they could not find a reading when taking my blood pressure, which resulted in the dramatic rushing on the trolley to try to 'revive' me. Turns out the blood pressure cuff and machine they were using were both faulty and as soon as they tried one that worked it transpired, I wasn't dying - I'd simply blacked out.

It wasn't a pleasant experience. I remembered really trying to fight hard to stay awake as I could hear their panic when they were speeding me through the corridor. It's all vague and I don't have a clue how long I was out, but I remember I couldn't see at one point and my breathing was awful until they gave me oxygen. I just couldn't fight it. I was exhausted from all the blood loss, but the situation from the outside probably looked much worse than it actually was.

They faffed over my care the next day. 'To scan or not to scan'? That was the question. They decided not, and I was eventually sent home with more meds and given an appointment to see a gynaecologist three months later (Sod that, have you met me before?) I got on the phone and begged for a cancellation and saw somebody within days. I couldn't bleed like that for 12 weeks. I'd have ended up with a permanent bed and paying council tax in that hospital, before long.

A couple of days later, a registrar gave me the option of a hysterectomy, a womb ablation (YUK) or suck it and see and until you decide here is a load more drugs. When after a few weeks I bled again, I stopped taking the meds and decided to 'suck it and see'. Do you learn that approach at medical school; I wonder? Thankfully, the bleeding stopped, and I have not bled since.

I am now officially menopausal, and I have the most wonderful hot flushes, to where I sweat and it drips down my face and back (and is an utter joy) but I would take this over that heavy bleeding, any day. So, thank you, chemotherapy, for pulling a blinder and screw you, ovaries, for trying to go on a comeback tour. Your days are now numbered. I think you'll find you are out for pasture, my friends.

Contrary to popular opinion, I've decided to replace the lost oestrogen with HRT in order to improve the quality of that I fought so hard to live for. Thank you to Dr. Louise Newson for opening my eyes and guiding me (through her website and app) into an educated post-menopausal future.

We're Going on a Boob Hunt.

A Parody by Sarah Vaughan

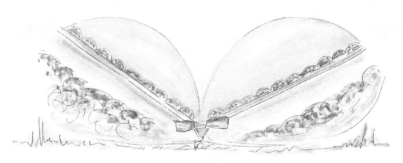

Written and illustrated by

Sarah Vaughan

in conjunction with #firstofthemonthcheckforalump

179

We're Going on a Boob Hunt

So, what to do now that episode was behind me? Lord knows; I can't sail through the weeks without a drama or a brainwave.

It was clear from my blogging that there is a lot of fear towards self-checking. I've had a lot of messages asking me how to check. People reporting that their boobs were so lumpy, they never know what to look for. Some telling me they were too scared to check.

What was obvious was I could do something about it. What wasn't obvious was how? Until I was doing the bedtime routine with my now crazy five-year-old and we were reading 'We're going on a Bear Hunt'. The idea to do a parody was born. Alas, like most of my brainwaves, I thought about it a lot before I did anything and actually put pen to paper. Master procrastinator, I had become, and I marvelled in how good my idea was and constantly visualised what it would look like. And still I did nothing.

I realised I'd become afraid of these ideas not working, looking good or reaching enough people. What is it they say? You won't regret what you've done, but only what you've not done? Or something like that. The idea of staying firmly shut in my head would not raise awareness with anyone. At least if I put something down and tried to share, it might help one person.

So 'We're Going on a Boob Hunt' was born. I wrote, illustrated and narrated my version of the parody and uploaded it to You Tube. I got lots of positive feedback from friends and family and they featured it in the local paper, and then nothing. No one was really interested.

Once again, I emailed This Morning, Loose Women, Lorraine, Granada Reports and look North West and got... nowhere, the buggers didn't want to know. I even tried to get in touch with Kylie.

It thrilled me that Michael Rosen himself re-tweeted it, but it never really got any interest. However, I'm super proud of it. Even if it's cheesy and my kids think it's hilarious that I've used my posh phone voice as the voice over but, it's not meant to be taken seriously. Its purpose is to jog a memory and provide a simple or easy way to remember how to check whilst you're in the bath or shower, or lying in bed.

I'm no Quentin Blake, but I liked the illustration and didn't know I had it in me. If you ever see it on social media, please share, it could save a life. If nothing else, you can laugh at my voice.

Trying to get home the message that breast cancer isn't just a lump isn't the easiest. People often shut down at the word cancer and don't want to know. Does ignorance always mean bliss? If it doesn't happen to you, it will happen to someone you know and love. That is just a fact. 1 in 8 women get Breast Cancer and running away from it won't change that. I think it's good to identity what the reasons are for not checking your boobs. Is it the 'optimism bias' that causes this, which is essentially a naïve belief that our chances of experiencing a negative event are lower than those of our friends or family? Or is it a type of bias like

'Confirmation Bias'? This is explained by someone who may seek to confirm that they won't get cancer because they don't fall into the age bracket and may choose to search or read information to back this theory up?

For example, when I was avoiding going for a smear, I researched the theory that having a smear can actually damage the tissue leading to abnormal cells developing in the cervix. I'd convinced myself, rather than it being a good thing to detect abnormal cells and therefore prevent further ill health; It would cause any abnormal cells. Sounds ridiculous, doesn't it? Of course, looking back, it was all based on fear.

Whatever the psychological reason, I now know personally for me, there has also been an element of avoidance and denial. So, I realise, these are some reasons I find it difficult to engage and muster support, but I won't stop. I am not after money or notoriety, I just want to spread the word, inform and educate, and hopefully give people the confidence to check. It could be the difference between someone needing chemotherapy or not, depending on how advanced it is. But I'm no psychologist. I find it really interesting to question the reasons behind our avoidance.

So please take the advice and check your boobs, go for that smear and pull your 'big girl' knickers up (or your y-fronts I don't care what you wear or identify in) and be self-aware. Ask yourself how much you know your own body and if you don't, start now. It's not too late. What follows are the visuals for your perusal, and there are no excuses...

Get on that boob hunt!

We're going on a boob hunt.
We're checking big and small ones.
We're not scared.
They are beautiful boobs.

Uh-uh! A mirror!
Standing naked in the mirror.
We have to check for changes.
It shouldn't take ages.

Oh no! We can't see through it.

Arms up! Eyes scan!
Arms down! Eyes scan!

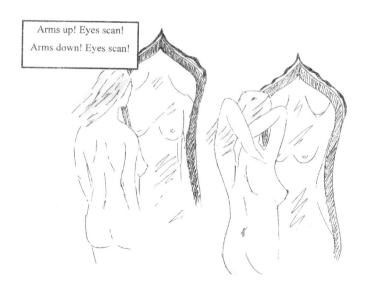

183

We're going on a boob hunt.
We're checking big and small ones.
We're not scared.
They are beautiful boobs.

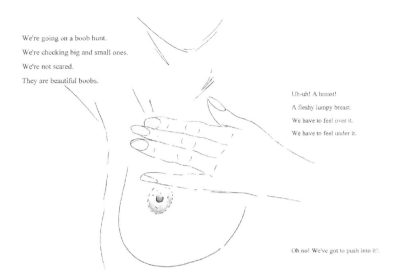

Uh-uh! A breast!
A fleshy lumpy breast.
We have to feel over it.
We have to feel under it.

Oh no! We've got to push into it!.

Squishy Squashy!
Squishy Squashy!
Squishy Squashy!

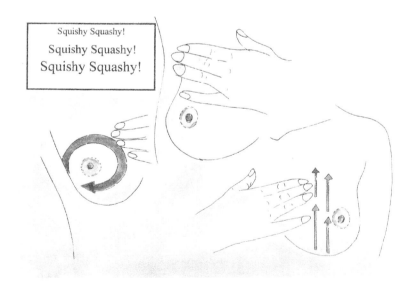

184

We're going on a boob hunt.

We're checking big and small ones.

We're not scared.

They are beautiful boobs.

Uh-uh! A nipple!

A small or massive nipple!

We can't have an oozy one,

We can't have a sunken one.

We can't have a sore one!

Mirror Check!

Feel check!

Squeeze check!

185

We're going on a boob hunt.

We're checking big and small ones.

We're not scared.

They are beautiful boobs.

Uh oh! A bed a large comfy bed!

We can't hide under it.

We can't jump over it.

We have to lie on it.

Arms up! Circle boob!
Arms up! Circle boob!

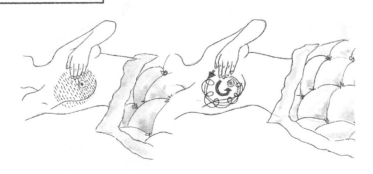

186

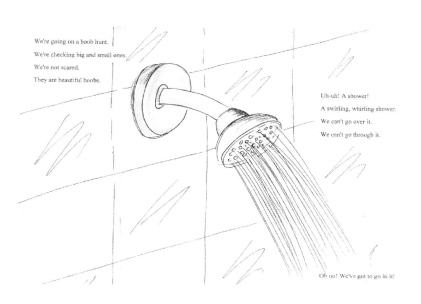

We're going on a boob hunt.

We're checking big and small ones.

We're not scared.

They are beautiful boobs.

Uh-uh! A shower!

A swirling, whirling shower.

We can't go over it.

We can't go through it.

Oh no! We've got to go in it!

Check squelch!

Poke squelch!

Massage squelch!

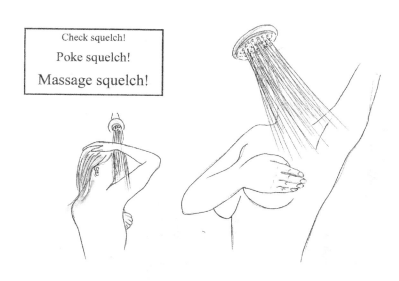

187

We're going on a boob hunt.

We're checking big and small ones.

We're not scared.

They are beautiful boobs.

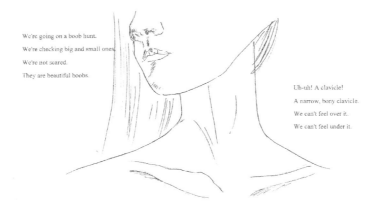

Uh-uh! A clavicle!

A narrow, bony clavicle.

We can't feel over it.

We can't feel under it.

Oh no! We've got to press around it!

Poke press!

Poke press!

Poke press!

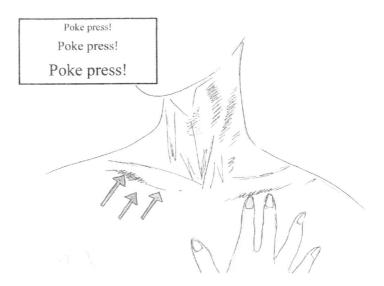

> **WHAT'S THAT!**
> It's a lump! A small dent!
> Is it soft! IT'S A WORRY!
>
> Quick! Check again.

Back to the clavicle! Press poke! Press poke! Press poke!

Back to the nipple! Mirror check! Squeeze Check! Feel check!

Back to the breast! Squishy Squashy! Squishy Squashy! Squishy Squashy!

Back to the mirror! Arms up! Eyes scan! Arms down! Eyes scan!

Back to the shower! Check squelch! Poke squelch! Massage squelch!

Back to the bed! Arms up! Circle boob! Arms up! Circle Boob!

Back to the pit! Poke prod! Poke prod! Poke prod!

191

Get the phone.
Call the GP.
Oh no! Line Busy
Call again.

Get referred
Scans taken
Tests Done
Results revealed

Phew…..Were not worrying like that again….It was only a cyst.
Thank God for the Boob Hunt and #firstofthemonthcheckforalump!

What? and Where Now?

At the time of writing, I never made it to This Morning sofa. I'd like to think, if I did, it would be with Holly and Phil and not Eamonn and Ruth. No offence guys, but I know Eamonn would probably say something inappropriate to my amazing knockers and Ruth would scowl at him and awareness would not be raised, just eyebrows. I now feel terrible for writing this as they have both been replaced!

I'm in a very lucky and fortunate place. I'm very healthy and happy with a lovely healthy family, a great house, fab friends and a job that pays well and I sometimes still enjoy.

I reflect a lot at this point. Whilst I'm no scientific researcher, I'm convinced stress contributed to me developing breast cancer. I'm not saying everyone who has hard times in their life will be prone, I just realise there were a lot of feelings, experiences and emotions that I had buried and not processed or resolved. It felt like I had a lot of negativity building up inside me and without unpicking these issues, as I was functionally ok, it was burdening me constantly. This is not me ending my story with self-blame or pity. I didn't have the emotional resources to deal with past traumatic events, and I now feel I'm a lot more self-aware. I realise I can't change the past, but I like to think I'm mindful of this for the future.

I'm hoping I can change others through writing this book and I plan to set up a charity to support families of people with cancer or who have survived cancer (specifically children). There are many charities out there that support children whose family members die from cancer, but not of those who survive but have suffered trauma. I want to offer a service that provides those family members with counselling, if they need it, or play therapy, or whatever that family feels they need to repair, grow and move forward.

I also want to push 'raising awareness' further too. I want to find companies who will display my posters on the back of their toilet doors or in their staff rooms. Why the hell not? Why wouldn't you want to see this message? It's not saying you're going to die, so don't have fun on my premises. It's saying love yourself and check your body. Stop fearing your own flesh and take responsibility for your health. Isn't that the first step towards self-love?

I'd love to go into schools and colleges and teach people that being self-aware of your mind and body is really important. And why your mind will play tricks on you and tell you 'it will never happen to me'. Because I can tell you it does, and it did. I survived it and luckily, I'm in a great place.

I often find worries about my health creeping up on me. I often catch myself having intrusive thoughts about my health, or the health of the people close to me, as a default, I guess. It's as if I'm trying to prepare myself for bad, or unexpected news. My subconscious mind feels like it's trying to protect me, in that if I am expecting it, it will hurt less, and I'll be more mentally prepared and less shocked. I know it doesn't work like that and I suppose I'm possibly describing some kind of 'post-traumatic stress' triggering these thoughts and feelings. It does not rule my life, but it is always there. I guess the fear will never go away, but I'm learning to live with it. Worrying about it won't change my destiny. It won't make me more prepared if it comes back, and it won't make it stay away either. I can only worry about the things I can change, and I can change my perspective on life. Some people may be alive, but they are not living. I don't live each day as if it's my last, but I try to put life in my days and not days in my life. I get complacent too, like everyone else I take things for granted, but not for long, as I reflect a lot on what I'm grateful for.

Yes, I have few frustrating leftovers from the surgery and treatment. They aren't life changing, but they are just an annoyance. They currently include:

- My eyes have never been the same. Always dry and itchy.
- I ache like a pensioner most mornings.
- I still have that annoying nasal drip.
- I struggle to motivate myself to exercise because the Diep surgery, where they sewed my stomach back together, feels strange and twinges sometimes. Or maybe it's just an excuse...
- I'm very impatient, I want things to happen yesterday.
- I get pins and needles down my right hand sometimes.
- I struggle to relax because it feels like time is too precious.
- My mouth often feels burnt.
- Still have osteopenia. (but it's not got any worse.)
- Awaiting more surgery to fix my boobs and Diep scar.

BUT!

I want to reiterate that I'm very, very grateful to still be alive, so although the above get me down, they aren't a big deal in the grand scheme of things. It is all about perspective, isn't it? If there is one thing this whole cancer experience/journey/ride (insert cheesy word here) has taught me, it is life is too short to be saying 'yes' to things to please others and to say YES to me. Do the things you keep putting off today because tomorrow or next year is not promised. Stop making excuses. And lastly, stop making excuses to check yourself. You now know how and why and what to do about it. If you find something, put down your phone and get off Dr Google and get to the GP. It is probably nothing, but you won't know if you don't get it checked out, and that's even if you find something other than the usual lumps and bumps. This applies to men, too. Men also have breast tissue and can get into the habit of checking, using the advice in this book. There are lots of resources available on the internet, if my voice is as annoying as my kids say it is! I'm now editing this in the middle of a pandemic. When COVID-19 is dominating our lives, fewer people are acting on intuition and getting to their GP. Worry will not shrink any cancers. Treatment will! Don't use Coronavirus as an excuse to avoid dealing with potential health problems of any kind. It is your right to seek treatment.

I hope you have been able to take something positive away from me sharing my story. It was important to be truthful and honest about how brutal this experience was for me. But the message is if I got through it, so can anyone. Please remember not everyone going through these shares the same experiences, when reflecting with Louisa my breast cancer nurse we discussed that I'd had a particularly difficult experience and my story isn't typical by any means. It's just real.

Please like my page on Facebook and share my posts. Thank you so much for reading this it means the world to me and I hope I've made you laugh and realise that a cancer diagnosis isn't the end of the world. I also hope I have been able to guide you through my journey with humour and I hope it helps yours.

Remember...

Boobs are for life, not just for Insta!

Before you go

I'm leaving you with some words of wisdom. I base this on my experiences and I'm sure some of these could apply to you if you experience cancer or want to support someone you know through cancer. It's not comprehensive, but it's from me to you. Navigating serious illness is tricky for everyone involved. Obviously this is not medical advice nor am I intending to tell you what to do. Hopefully, these tips will make life a little easier.

If it's you....

- Don't 'Dr Google' symptoms/answers, it will mash your head.
- Accept help from anyone who offers (providing you vaguely like them).
- Do not blame yourself for your diagnosis. If scientists don't know, how come you do.
- Don't wallow... self-pity isn't attractive, even when you're bald.
- It's ok to feel sad and scared. Just not all the time.
- Think positively. There is always something to be positive about. Honestly.
- Don't expect too much after treatment. The chemo is busy killing bad cells, the good ones are trying to keep up.

- Accept legal drugs like anti-sickness! Or anything else, make the most of it.

- Write what you need to take and when... your brain is about to be fried and you will forget.

- Write what you have taken and when... your brain is being fried and you won't remember.

- Nana nap when you need to. Your body needs the rest, and you have an excellent excuse.

- If people say what can I do to help? Tell them. Clean/cook/childcare. They would much prefer to help than send flowers.

- Get some counselling, talk it through. Cry it through. It's essential to offload.

- Book yourself in for a treatment. Boost your immunity.

- Eat well and drink lots of water. If you don't have an appetite for a salad during treatment, eat a donut if that's what you want.

- Join a support group if that's your thing. If it isn't, then don't. These are your rules.

-

If it's someone you care about like a friend or family member:

- Drop round a care package. Be thoughtful rather than frivolous.

- Don't worry about saying the wrong thing. Just be you.

- Share your concerns and worries or problems as you would have. Yes, they may not compare to having cancer, but they are real for you. We want to hear them.

- Be polite but always be honest (it's refreshing) people pretend you look well when you don't.

- Keep in contact. Having cancer can be lonely. Even if it is sharing a meme.

- Don't take offence if they don't reply. They are knackered. It's not personal.

- Do expect that they won't feel like themselves. Do expect this may make you sad.

-

If you are the carer:

- Accept help. Share the load. Accept hand-outs/advice/food parcels.
- Eat well and get some sleep. You can't pour from an empty cup.
- Do something for you. Gym/Golf/Read/Knit/Hand-gliding. Whatever floats your boat?
- Cry if you need to. You are human. Just don't flood the house.
- Remember to breathe. It's kind of essential...
- Don't feel guilty if you're struggling. You will struggle at some point.
- Get some counselling. Yes, you...you may benefit.
- Be overwhelmed...just don't pack up and live there.

Acknowledgements

A massive thank you for all the texts, gifts, cards, prayers, visits, meals and favours I received during my treatment. I was truly touched by every single act of support during this time and there are too many to mention personally and it would really upset me if I missed anyone out.

Thank you to Donna who helped me with my first edit and gave me the confidence to publish. She also taught me about commas after all these years.

Louisa my Macmillan nurse was brilliant. She is still brilliant. Louisa works long hours but always there for me whenever I call. She has never been pushy or over sympathetic. She is calm, knowledgeable and caring. I'm sure the breast unit would clone her if they could. Thank you, Louisa.

The staff and volunteers at the Lilac centre and Burney breast unit at St. Helens hospital work so professionally to offer a caring approach and I want to thank those who made my experience as positive as it could be.

Thank you to Lena Chagla my breast cancer surgeon. What a woman, and the command she has over everyone without being abrupt or condescending. She is a force.

Dr.Ommen Koshy, my plastic surgeon. Dedicated and skilful. Thank you for your calm expertise and emotional support when I felt broken before surgery.

All the medical staff I came across throughout my treatment. You are all angels. Thank you for your tender care and humility. We are very lucky to have the NHS and you make it so special.

Another thanks to my close and extended family, especially my children who have had to compromise throughout. We may be a blended family, but you are my world and the reason I fought so hard.

A huge thank you to anyone who has ever shared, or liked my blog. It's not easy to get the message out there, but with your help and encouragement I will continue to spread the word.

#firstofthemonthcheckforalump

About the Author

Sarah is still enjoying teaching Art and PSHE in a unit in St Helens for students with complex and medical needs.

Currently, she is still unconfidently blogging and passionate about trying to raise awareness of checking boobs and being body aware. She says she feels like her tech. skills still need to improve to keep up with the changing platforms and how they operate, but she is getting there!

Her charity now has a name, but it is very much in its infancy and fundraising ideas are being explored in the hope of post Covid-19 restrictions being lifted soon. It will then be all systems go, and hopefully her dream of being in a position to signpost and fund support for children and families struggling through cancer can be achieved.

Most importantly, the health and happiness of her family remain her priority. The crazy 3 year old is now 7 and still keeping the family entertained. Sarah is excited about the future, having fun and making memories and still lives by the motto: "Put life in your days, not days in your life".

Printed in Great Britain
by Amazon